AUTHOR OF THE JESUS CREED: LOVING GOD, LOVING OTHERS

SCOT MCKNIGHT

40 DAYS

LIVING
THE
JESUS
CREED

Updated edition—now includes a study guide by
Fr. Kevin Maney

PARACLETE PRESS
BREWSTER, MASSACHUSETTS

40 *Days Living the Jesus Creed*

2014 First and Second Printing This Edition

Copyright © 2008 by Scot McKnight

ISBN: 978-1-61261-524-0

Published in association with the literary agency of Daniel Literary Group, 1701 Kingsbury Drive, Suite 100, Nashville, TN 37215.

Unless otherwise indicated, Scripture quotations are from the *New Revised Standard Version* of the Bible, copyright © 1989 by the Division of Christian Education of the National Council of Churches of Christ in the USA. Used by permission. All rights reserved.

Scripture quotations marked *Today's New International Version* are taken from the Holy Bible, Today's New International Version™ TNIV®. Copyright © 2001, 2005 by International Bible Society®. All rights reserved worldwide.

Scripture quotations marked *The Message* are taken from *THE MESSAGE*. Copyright © 1993, 1994, 1995, 1996, 2000, 2001, 2002. Used by permission of NavPress Publishing Group.

The Paraclete Press name and logo (dove on cross) is a trademark of Paraclete Press, Inc.

The first edition of this book was catalog with the Library of Congress as follows:
Library of Congress Cataloging-in-Publication Data
McKnight, Scot.
    40 days living the Jesus creed / Scot McKnight.
        p. cm.
ISBN-13: 978-1-55725-577-8
    1. Christian life--Biblical teaching. 2. Devotional literature. I. Title.
BS680.C47M35 2008
248.4—dc22   2007049368

10 9 8 7 6 5 4 3 2

Published by Paraclete Press
Brewster, Massachusetts
www.paracletepress.com

Printed in the United States of America

For the Jesus Creed Blog Community

hosted daily at

www.jesuscreed.org

Fine and faithful Christian conversationalists

CONTENTS

INTRODUCTION

Recently my wife, Kris, and I attracted hummingbirds into our backyard to feed on our assortment of feeders and flowers. Throughout a weekend marked by perfect weather, Kris and I sat on our screened porch and read and talked and visited with family and ate our meals together. We learned something that weekend about those little marvels called hummingbirds: they eat constantly. My estimation is they visit our feeders and flowers forty or fifty times a day. Instead of gobbling up an entire bottle of nectar in one sitting, hummers poke their spindly, needle-nosed beaks and extendible tongues to extract nectar from plants and feeders all day long.

Herein lies a parable for us today: many of us live as if we were designed to eat like lions, as if one big meal (Sunday) is enough to sustain us for the week. Not so. Followers of Jesus are more like hummingbirds than lions. We need a steady diet of spiritual nectar if we are to live the kind of life Jesus asks us to live. That life I summarized in a book called *The Jesus Creed*, an expression I use for Jesus' double commandment to love God and to love others.

40 Days Living the Jesus Creed extends what we explored in *The Jesus Creed* into other passages in the Gospels. We then extend the ongoing life of the Jesus Creed into the rest of the New Testament to discover how the Jesus Creed undergirds the Sermon on the Mount, the Love Chapter of the apostle Paul, and the core moral teachings of James (brother of Jesus), Peter, and the apostle John. Because we need a steady diet of Jesus Creed nectar, we have in this book forty short chapters. Exploring how the Jesus Creed lives in other writers of the New Testament offers you and me ongoing reminders, daily feedings as it were, of what is most important—learning to put into practice what it means to love God and to love others.

When I wrote *The Jesus Creed,* I had fond hopes that it would catch on. Yet its success continues to surprise me. Originally I included a concluding chapter to *The Jesus Creed* that revealed how significant the Jesus Creed was to the early Christians, but my editor thought that the book ended where it should have and that a description of the ongoing life of the Jesus Creed could wait until another time. That time is now.

We learn to love God and love others only if we dedicate ourselves to an ongoing commitment to live the Jesus Creed daily. So, my prayer is that by spreading out these two themes over forty days, with a new exploration each day, we will expose ourselves to the potent grace of God's love sufficiently to become more loving.

One more reminder. Neither *40 Days Living the Jesus Creed* nor *The Jesus Creed* can be as effective as they are intended to be if we do not commit ourselves to reciting the Jesus Creed in the morning, in the evening, and anytime during the day that it comes to mind. Here's why: this was the moral creed of Jesus and the earliest Christians. What was an early Christian daily recital fell away as the church moved away from Judaism. So it is our prayer that the daily recital of the Jesus Creed will find its way back into the daily practice of Christians today. Once again, here is the Jesus Creed as found in Mark 12:29–31:

"Hear, O Israel: the Lord our God, the Lord is one; you shall love the Lord your God with all your heart, and with all your soul, and with all your mind, and with all your strength." The second is this, "You shall love your neighbor as yourself." There is no other commandment greater than these.

PART 1

The Jesus Creed

The Jesus Creed exhorts us to see that the most important commandments in the entire Bible are two: to love God and to love others. All the other commandments and prohibitions—and there are 611 others—derive from one of these two most important commands.

DAY 1

The Most Important Commandments

*Hear, O Israel: The L*ORD *our God,*
*the L*ORD *is one.*
*You shall love the L*ORD *your God*
with all your heart,
and with all your soul,
and with all your might.
—Deuteronomy 6:4–5

We need to remind ourselves daily of what is most important: our primary relationship to God is love. We love God in response to God's great love for us. So important is it to love God, that God tells Israel that they are to remind themselves of their need to love God by developing a sacred rhythm of reciting the following words daily: "Hear, O Israel: The LORD our God, the LORD is one. You shall love the LORD your God with all your heart, and with all your soul, and with all your might. Keep these words that I am commanding you today in your heart." These words from the sixth chapter of Deuteronomy are called the *Shema* because the first word of these lines, "Hear," is *shema* in Hebrew.

IMPORTANT WORDS

Notice God's next words: "Recite [these words] to your children and talk about them when you are at home and when you are away, when you lie down and when you rise. Bind them as a sign on your hand, fix them as an emblem on your forehead, and write them on the doorposts of your house and on your gates."

Loving God was *the subject matter* for an Israelite's whole day. All of life was about loving God with every ounce of one's being. This was so important that they were to teach their children. So important that they were to recite the *Shema* when they were at home and when they were at work or on vacation. So important that they were to recite them when they got up and when they went to bed, which is the liturgical church's catalyst for morning prayers and vespers prayers. So important that they were to write them on scraps of papyrus, roll them up, and place them in little leather pouches, and strap the pouches to the forehead and arm. So important that they were to write them on the doorways to their homes. So important that they were to write them on the portals to their cities and villages.

That's how important it was to remind themselves to love God.

But Jesus said this was not enough.

IMPORTANT AMENDMENT

When Jesus was asked by a budding intellectual, who was no doubt more concerned about a theological debate and an intellectual puzzle than how to walk with God, what was the most important commandment of them all, Jesus recited the *Shema* he had learned from his mother and father as a little boy. Jesus began to answer the man's question in typical fashion. But instead of stopping at Deuteronomy 6, where the intellectual thought Jesus would end, Jesus amended the *Shema* by adding the italicized words of a long-ignored verse in Leviticus (19:18): "You shall not take vengeance or bear a grudge against any of your people, but *you shall love your neighbor as yourself*: I am the LORD." The one God of Israel, the LORD, not only summons his people to love God but also summons them to love their neighbors as themselves. Jesus amended the sacred *Shema* of Israel by adding "love your neighbor as yourself" to what was to be recited daily.

IMPORTANT RHYTHM

About five years ago I bundled up the courage to do what Jesus did. I decided I would say the *Shema* as Jesus did—at least twice a day (morning and evening)—and I would also say it as often as it came to my mind throughout the day. (Sometimes I say it thirty or forty times.) I also decided I would recite the *Shema* in the Jesus form—what I soon began to call the "Jesus Creed." That is, I'd say what Jesus said in Mark 12:29–31:

> "Hear, O Israel: the Lord our God, the Lord is one; you shall love the Lord your God with all your heart, and with all your soul, and with all your mind, and with all your strength." The second is this, "You shall love your neighbor as yourself." There is no other commandment greater than these.

I have been saying this nonstop for five years, much to the moral danger of my own life! To remind ourselves in a sacred rhythm that our central tasks are to love God and to love others is to keep in mind something that is more challenging than anything in life. It is one thing to do what seems to be right or good and just; it is another thing to love God and to love others—all day long with every ounce of our being.

I challenge you to make this your sacred rhythm.

Facing this day:
Recite the Jesus Creed throughout the day.

Scriptural focus:
"Hear, O Israel: the Lord our God, the Lord is one;
you shall love the Lord your God with all your
heart, and with all your soul, and with all your
mind, and with all your strength." The second is
this, "You shall love your neighbor as yourself."
There is no other commandment greater than these.
—Mark 12:29–31

Loving God

"You shall love the Lord your God
with all your heart,
and with all your soul,
and with all your mind,
and with all your strength."
—Mark 12:30

L oving God is a great idea until you try to love God all day long. It is much easier to want to love God or even to say we will love God than it is to love God when yawning cracks of life begin to suck us downward.

To love God means to yearn for, to pray for, and work for what glorifies God and what puts God in God's place in your life. The Jesus Creed summons us to love God with every ounce of our being—heart, soul, mind, and strength. To love God this way means to offer to God all that we are and to enjoy God's presence.

David Gill writes of two kinds of love: table-love, which is the love of fellowship and communion, and cross-love, which is the love seen in sacrifice and devotion. We might add that we find his first kind of love, table-love, through his second kind of love, cross-love. We could say that we find delightful communion with God by giving ourselves to God just as we find delightful communion with a friend or lover by giving ourselves to the other. Jesus calls us to the cross-love of God by giving to God our heart, soul, mind, and strength—and on the other side, we find table-love with God.

GIVE GOD YOUR HEART

The "heart" is the center of one's *affections*. Think of what you love, what motivates you. Perhaps it is your spouse, your children, your best friend, your job, your hobby, or your travel plans. Give what comes to mind to God by gently offering those affections and persons and ambitions today.

GIVE GOD YOUR SOUL

The "soul" is the center of our *spirituality*. Think of your relationship to God, of what you deem most significant in your spiritual life, of the core of your life. It might begin with prayer or with personal time with God or with your evening time of meditation or with

Bible reading or even with your spiritual vocation or gift. Perhaps it is a daily walk into the mountains or along a body of water during which time you commune with God. Give what comes to mind to God by offering your very soul to God.

GIVE GOD YOUR MIND

The "mind" is the center of our rationality. Think of what you believe, of how you think, of your need for logic, of your need for making sense. Think of how precious your brain is and how it controls all you do. Now give your mind—all you will think about today—to God.

GIVE GOD YOUR STRENGTH

The word "strength" refers to our whole being, our strength and our might and our wealth and all our resources. Coming as this does at the end of a list, we are led to a climactic point: "Love God *with all you've got!*" This word "strength" includes heart, soul, and mind, and might be best translated with boldface: "that is, ***with everything!***" Think of your body, your ambition, your dreams, your bank account, your insurance policy, and your talents.

To love is to give of ourselves; to love God is to give God all we are and all we have. Give your "strength"—in all you do today—to God.

When I was five years old, my great-aunt Lela Schmacker took this hyperactive kid to a large department store in St. Louis. As we entered the store, she made me an incredible offer: "Scot, you can have anything you want in the whole store. Shop around and just let me know what you would like. I'll buy it for you." Don't imagine that I was like those folks today who get fifteen minutes to fill up their shopping carts. My aunt let me choose one thing, but it was anything I could find in Stix, Baer and Fuller.

Both my mother and father were with me and, to their credit, while they coached me on some ideas, they let me make up my mind. They thought a tent might be a nice idea, and it wouldn't surprise me that they thought this was a good idea because it would get me out of the house and protect their sanity. I walked around and looked at lots of things, but I was a baseball nut, and so I chose a first baseman's mitt. Wondering if I might be overextending myself, I also asked my Aunt Lela if I could also have a new baseball. Knowing that she was being let off easy, she said, "Sure."

I've thought about this event a number of times in my life. I imagine that we, like my great-aunt, are inviting

God into the department store of our life and we are offering to God to take whatever he wants. There is a difference: the "one" thing God wants from us is *all* of us. No, in fact, he wants more than all of us: he wants our *love.* If we give God our love, we give God all our "strength."

———

Facing this day:
Offer your love today to God.

Scriptural focus:
"Hear, O Israel: the Lord our God, the Lord is one; you shall love the Lord your God with all your heart, and with all your soul, and with all your mind, and with all your strength."
—Mark 12:29–30

Loving Others

"You shall love your neighbor as yourself."
—Mark 12:31

L oving others is a great idea until "Mr. or Ms. Other" happens to be a person you don't like. If we are honest with ourselves, the exhortation to "love your neighbor as yourself" slides quickly into a decision to love someone we like or someone just like us. So, for example, in the world of Jesus, loving God naturally meant doing the Torah. Doing the Torah involved maintaining some firm boundary lines between the holy and the profane, the Israelite and the Gentile, the clean and the unclean. So, the commandment to love your *neighbor* as yourself became for (too) many persons little more than loving one's holy, Israelite, clean neighbors. The profane, Gentile, and unclean person was erased from the dictionary definition of "neighbor." Jesus redefined the word *neighbor*.

We might say that Jesus' primary sparring partners, the Pharisees, practiced a "love of Torah" that created boundary lines between neighbors and non-neighbors. Jesus turned that Pharisee expression around and believed in a "Torah of love" that crossed boundaries by redefining the word "neighbor." And to make loving one's neighbor central to life, Jesus picked up the central moral creed of his Jewish world, the *Shema*, and amended it. He added "love your neighbor as yourself" to the *Shema*, which urged Israelites to recite daily these words: "Love the Lord your God with all your heart, and with all your soul, and with all your mind, and with all your strength." Jesus' amendment created a moral creed that summoned Israel to love God *and to love their neighbors as themselves.*

A scribe asked Jesus how to gain eternal life. Jesus, ever the good teacher, asked him what the Torah teaches. After proving to Jesus that he understood the Jesus Creed, that the two central commands of God's Torah were to love God and love others, that scribe asked Jesus another question. This time, though, the scribe revealed that he was not yet ready for the revolutionary nature of the Jesus Creed he had so glibly coughed up. He asked Jesus, probably with a little sniff of snobbery, "Who is my neighbor?" (Luke 10:29). Jesus answered with the parable of the good Samaritan (Luke 10:30–37). That clever parable revealed that the real question was not "Who is my neighbor?"—a question that permits one to create boundary lines—but "To whom should I be neighborly?"

The Jesus Creed calls us to neighbor-love—regardless of who the neighbor might be.

BE PREPARED FOR THE UNPREDICTABLE

You cannot determine in advance to whom you will need to act in neighbor-love. Neither can you determine what kind of love you will show. I have joked for years that my education prepared me best to exit my front door on Saturday mornings, to summon my neighbors into my front yard as I stand on the porch, and then to give them a short exposition of a passage from the Greek New Testament. The only problem is that no one would come! We all like to do what we are good at, but my neighbors need something other than what I have to offer in explaining the New Testament.

To discern what prompts neighbor-love, we need to develop eyes that see and ears that hear needs. Sometimes our neighbors need us to mow grass or shovel snow or bring in the mail or look after a dog. They might need us to take them to pick up their car, or they might request a lift to the doctor's office. What neighbor-love does is never predictable. Often neighbor-love interrupts our schedule, annoying us more than we care to admit, and calls us to abandon our plans. But our eyes will reveal and our ears will hear the needs of our neighbors if we learn to live the Jesus Creed.

RESPOND TO NEEDS, NOT LABELS

In Jesus' parable of the good Samaritan, the priest and the Levite, who both knew and observed their Torah, saw the man sprawled out on the path and thought he was dead. A corpse was impure, and the Torah taught priests not to defile themselves with corpse impurity unless the dead person was their nearest kin (Leviticus 21:1–4). So they passed him by. In effect, then, the priest and the Levite were doing what the Torah said. But that wasn't enough for Jesus. Someone as desperate as a man abandoned on the road had a need, and needs come before labels and purity laws. This corpse was labeled "unclean," and the priest and the Levite, in Jesus' comic parable, respond to the label instead of the need. The Samaritan, who in stereotyped categories shouldn't have been the one to respond, responded to the need and ignored the label.

We are like the priest and the Levite far more often than we care to admit. We may choose not to stop our journey to respond to persons because of their ethnicity, their economic status, their clothing, their age, or their body piercings or tattoos. Sometimes we respond negatively to an immigrant's accent or country of origin, or we may fall prey to stereotypes about such persons. Sometimes we walk away from persons because of their disease or their rumored sins. Neighbor-love, as Jesus teaches it and practices it, crosses those boundaries because it responds to needs, not labels.

Two of the biggest challenges of living the Jesus Creed are these: learning to see and hear the needs of the one who happens to be my neighbor and learning to discern when and how to respond. These are the challenges of the Jesus Creed to neighbor-love.

Jesus' word is to us: "Go and do likewise."

Facing this day:
Love the one who happens to be
your neighbor today.

Scriptural focus:
*"Which of these three [priest, Levite, Samaritan],
do you think, was a neighbor to the man who fell
into the hands of the robbers?" [The scribe] said,
"The one who showed him mercy." Jesus said to
him, "Go and do likewise."*
—Luke 10:36–37

PART 2

The God of the Jesus Creed

The Jesus Creed does not appear out of thin air. The commands to love God and to love others derive from the love of God: that is, the love of the Father and the Son and the Spirit for one another, and the love of God for us. The origin of the Jesus Creed is found in God.

Facing God Today

"Everyone who loves is born
of God and knows God.
Whoever does not love does not
know God, for God is love."
—1 John 4:7b–8

The Bible talks about the face of God often. It doesn't teach that God has a physical face like ours, one with a long, white beard or long, flowing white hair or makeup over the eyes and a touch of perfume at the ear. The Bible uses the word "face" for God because the Bible speaks so often of our relationship to God. And face is how we express our most important relationships, our "face-to-face" relationships. God's face is how God relates to you and me. Perhaps you have heard this famous line from Numbers 6 sung so often by a choir or recited in your church that you miss its significance:

The Lord make his face to shine upon you, and be gracious to you; the Lord lift up his countenance upon you, and give you peace.

This prayer of Moses summons Israel to experience the healing glory of gazing into the face of God. What the Bible is telling us is that God's face is turned toward us with divine delight in who we are, and we are invited to turn our faces toward God to find grace and peace.

For us to be empowered by that face, we have to turn our face to God by gazing at God and by talking to God. If we fake it, we offer to God nothing but a façade. If we face God honestly by offering our true face to God, we discover in the face of God the face of love. We discover that "God is love."

The Jesus Creed begins in the face of God, for until we see in the face of God the love God has for us, we will not find the strength to love God, to love ourselves, or to love others. This love begins in the face of God.

THE FACE OF INVITATION

I know and love the face of my wife, Kris. I don't have to ask permission to look at her. When I look at Kris I see the fourth-grader I met when we jumped on a trampoline together; I see the teenager I fell in love with at fifteen; I see the college student I married; I see the mother of our children; and I see the psychologist who shows the face of healing; I see the face of one who delights when hummingbirds feed in our yard. But most of all, I see the face of the one who has loved me. It's all there. In her face.

God also wants us to gaze at his face. God made you and me with a face designed to face God.

You don't have to know some special code to dial up God's face; you don't have to attend one particular church or have an education or live in a favored country. To face God, you just have to be human, someone with a heart and a mind and a face and some fingers and legs and toes. You don't have to utter special words or do a specified number of good deeds to earn a glimpse of the face of God. You just have to be you and turn your unique face toward God.

SEE GOD'S FACE AS WHO GOD IS

The apostle John says as much in the fourth chapter of his first letter when he says, "*God is love*, and those who abide in love abide in God, and God abides in them." John does not tell us that God *has* love or that God often *acts* in love or that God *relates* to us in love—though each of those is true. God *is* love; that is, God is *defined* by love. God is love the way grass is green and the sky is blue and a flower is aromatic and a line is straight and a circle is round and a favorite chair is comfortable. Love isn't God's part-time vocation, as if God is sometimes holy and other times loving. God is love, always and forever. And, the face of God's love is his unconditional regard for who we are and sacred concern for everything we do.

SEE IN GOD'S FACE THE JESUS CREED

The Jesus Creed that shapes this book flows from the face of God's gracious love. We learn to live the Jesus Creed when we begin to face God. Sometimes, like Adam and Eve, we hide our faces from God, hoping God might not find us as God strolls through the garden. We hide from God for all kinds of reasons: Perhaps we did not learn to love well from our parents or family, or perhaps we have experienced or are still in a deeply wounding relationship, or perhaps we are tired and weary from seeking intimacy. Such experiences can turn our face from God. But, facing God heals us and empowers us to become lovers of God and lovers of others.

———————

Facing this day:
Face God today and discover the face of love.

Scriptural focus:
"The LORD *make his face to shine upon you, and be gracious to you."*
—Numbers 6:25

The Divine Dance

"The Father and I are one.
Believe [my] works,
so that you may know and understand that
the Father is in me
and I am in the Father."
—John 10:30, 38

At the center of the Jesus Creed is the *Shema*, and at the center of the *Shema* is the God of love, and at the center of the God of love is the word "one"—and that word "one" is a dance. Let me explain briefly. When Jesus said in John's tenth chapter that he and the Father were "one," every Jew who heard him thought of the *Shema*: "Hear, O Israel! The Lord our God, the Lord is *one*." Now Jesus was claiming that he and the Father were *one*. So somehow there were "two in one," and, as the church gradually began to comprehend, there were actually "three in one." The Jesus Creed derives from this "three-in-oneness of God."

How are the three "one"? Here are Jesus' own words: "the Father is *in* me and I am *in* the Father." The oneness of the Father and the Son is the oneness of *mutual indwelling of one another*. Now, if we add to the Father and the Son the third person of the Trinity, the Holy Spirit, we arrive at something distinct to our Christian faith: the Father and the Son and the Spirit are one because they indwell one another. They interpenetrate one another so deeply that they are one. This "oneness" is often called by theologians the "dance of the Trinity." God is almost, to quote C.S. Lewis, "if you think me not irreverent, a kind of dance." God is, to change the image only slightly, the dance of rope in the Celtic knot.

The same theologians often call this oneness of God the *perichoresis*, a Greek word referring to mutual indwelling. To say the three are one is to say the one God is a community of mutually indwelling persons where each person delightfully dances with the other in endless holy love. This perichoretic dance is the love of the persons of the Trinity for each other—the Father for the Son and the Spirit, and the Son for the Father and the Spirit, and the Spirit for the Father and the Son. Theologians and philosophers remind us that this perichoretic love is the origin, the tone, and the standard for all the love in the universe. There is no other love than God's love.

The mutual love of the Father, Son, and Spirit form the pattern for the Jesus Creed. The Jesus Creed summons each of us to dance the dance of the Trinity.

DANCING

Once, Kris persuaded me to take dance lessons. To be sure, some might not call "disco lessons" real dance lessons, but it was the days of *Saturday Night Fever*, and I went along with her idea and did my best. It became rather obvious that I simply could not dance, so Kris quit trying to persuade me, and I was quite happy to return to something I enjoy: watching others dance. I do marvel at how well some people can dance. Their entire bodies seem to be overwhelmed by the music and the beat and the meaning of the words. Somehow the body moves in such a way that the music begins to take on bodily form. We might say that the dance incarnates the music, just as the Son incarnates the dance of the Trinity.

God is love. The music of God is love. Anyone who loves God and loves others is dancing, whether he or she knows it or not, to the divine dance. To love is to walk onto the divine dance floor.

So when Jesus calls us to love God and to love others, he invites us to join him in the divine dance of the Trinity. Perhaps the greatest news in the universe is that we have been invited to dance on God's dance floor. We don't have to worry about whether or not someone will invite us to this dance; we don't even have to worry about whom we might dance with; and we don't have to dance well to join in God's dance.

Love isn't something we produce. Love, like dancing, is surrendering to the music on the divine dance floor. We may need to remind ourselves of the words from the previous chapter, because these words express the music of God: "God is love, and those who abide in love abide in God, and God abides in them" (1 John 4:16).

———————

Facing this day:
Join the dance of God today.

Scriptural focus:
"But if I do [these good works], even though you do not believe me, believe the works, so that you may know and understand that the Father is in me and I am in the Father."
—John 10:38

DAY 6

Eikons of Love

So God created humankind in his image,
in the image of God he created them;
male and female he created them.
—Genesis 1:27

God made you to love God, to love yourself, and to love others. We sometimes forget that we were put on Planet Earth to love.

Kris and I once tried to drive our rental car from Venice to our hotel in Florence, Italy. We got up early that morning and everything went wonderfully until we got to Florence. In spite of the many, many warnings we had been given that driving in Florence is impossible, we thought we could follow the directions given to us and find our hotel. After one hour and forty-five minutes of driving in and out of streets that were not on our map, turning onto streets that did not appear to us to be named, and losing nearly all the sanity we had left, we pulled over near a big river—the Arno, I believe, but at that time it hardly mattered—and simultaneously asked ourselves this simple question: "Why are we in Italy, anyway?" Our answer: "To see the hillsides of Tuscany, to smell the air of the land, to taste the food, to experience the evening sunsets, and to enjoy what we like the most: wandering in and out of countryside Italian villages."

Kris asked me the big question: "Do you really want to see Florence?" I said, "Not if you don't want to." "That settles it," Kris said. "Let's go find a hotel in San Gimignano." Suddenly, we weren't lost. We turned our backs on Florence and drove to the picturesque medieval village and filled the rest of our week with what we most enjoy.

KNOW YOURSELF AS AN *EIKON*

Sometimes we lose sight of why we are here. We are, Moses tells us in the first chapter of the Bible, made in God's image. The Greek translations of the Hebrew Bible translate the word behind "image" with the word *eikon*, and this word *eikon* is my favorite translation of the Hebrew word for "image" (*tselem*). We are, the Bible tells us, *eikons*. Knowing we are *eikons* empowers us to love. To be an *eikon* is to be given the capacity to enter into the perichoresis—the mutual indwelling of love of the three persons of the Trinity—and to learn to love. The Jesus Creed—Jesus' commandments to love God and to love others as ourselves—perfectly expresses what God created an *eikon* to do.

KNOW WHAT *EIKONS* ARE FOR

We love, so the first three chapters of Genesis inform us, in four directions. We love God, we love ourselves, we love others, and we love the good world God has given to us. So, when Adam and Eve chose to go against God's good plan, they "cracked" that *eikon*. To be a cracked *eikon* means that our love is distorted in all four directions: we don't love God as we can, we don't love ourselves as we should, we don't love others as we ought, and we don't love the good world God gave us as we are designed.

The gospel is designed to restore us in all four directions—in our love for God, for ourselves, for others, and the world. This is why Jesus is the perfect *Eikon*: he loves God, loves himself, loves others, and lovingly observes and cares for God's world. Paul tells us that we are summoned to the horizon to see the "light of the gospel of the glory of Christ, who is the image of God" (2 Corinthians 4:4). And even more important, he tells us that when we gaze on this perfect *Eikon*, we will be "transformed into the same image (*eikon*) from one degree of glory to another; for this comes from the Lord, the Spirit" (3:18).

Think about this today, because we sometimes forget why we are here: you and I are *eikons*. *Eikons* reflect and manifest God to the world around them. They do this when they love God, love themselves, love others, and love the good world God has given to them. But we only glow as *eikons* when we love.

It is so easy to get lost in our plans, in our hopes, in our worries, and in our busyness. What we need is to come to our senses. We need to pull off the road and ask ourselves, "What are we here for?" That is a question worth answering, and it is answered with utter clarity when we realize who we are. We are *eikons*, designed by God to live the Jesus Creed.

Facing this day:
You are an *eikon* made to love God, love yourself, love others, and love the world.

Scriptural focus:
"And all of us, with unveiled faces, seeing the glory of the Lord as though reflected in a mirror, are being transformed into the same image from one degree of glory to another; for this comes from the Lord, the Spirit."
—2 Corinthians 3:18

DAY 7

Midnight Mary's Love

*But the L*ORD *God called to the man,*
and said to him,
"Where are you?"
—Genesis 3:9

In Freeport, Illinois, one woman's name, as it was known at the street level, was "Midnight Mary." A boyhood friend of mine, James Vanoosting, told her story in a redemptive way in his novel *Walking Mary.* Midnight Mary's son never came home from World War II, but Midnight Mary never gave up hope that her one-and-only-son might still be alive. So, for years—and I am an eyewitness to her routine—she walked to the train station in Freeport, Illinois, and watched as each passenger got off the train. "Maybe," she mumbled to herself daily, "just maybe my son will return home today." I remember her still going to the train station in the 1960s. We all thought her son was dead, but she hoped against hope. The love she had for her son was boundless, and no matter how much your heart aches for

Midnight Mary, she remains for everyone from Freeport a visible symbol of persistence.

You might give up on yourself, but God doesn't and won't. His love is persistent, and it this kind of love that creates the Jesus Creed.

Jesus once told a story of a Midnight Mary–like image for God's love for us in the parable of the prodigal son (Luke 15:11–32). Perhaps today we can be empowered to love God and others by listening one more time to Jesus' story. This parable is a living illustration of God's loving persistence and searching to renew fellowship when God asked a hiding-behind-the-trees Adam: "Where are you?" The implication is clear: God wasn't going anywhere; God was waiting persistently for Adam simply to come out from behind the tree. And only by coming out to meet the face of love would Adam find healing.

OUR FATHER RISKS

The prodigal son's story goes like this: A father had an estate and some servants and two sons. The younger son, who typified in Judaism the rebellious son, got it in his head that he had had enough with the Torah-observant life. So, knowing enough about inheritance laws to make himself dangerous to an intact family, he approached his father with *chutzpah*: "Can I have my share—thirty-three percent—of the estate now?" Not only did the son's request cut deeply into the father's own income base, but also the son's behavior shamed the father in front of all his peers. The father, however, loved his son and risked letting his son do as he wished. Loving God, Jesus tells us, is a personal choice. God won't force his way onto his children.

Most historians agree that the father's behavior here is unusual: what we expect of the father is a rebuke and discipline, the way you and I might say, "Go to your room and get your act together." But this father permitted the son to leave, to ruin himself, to lose all his money, and even to eat farm food for animals. And he allowed the son to wait it out until he returned—and that is what the son did.

OUR FATHER WAITS

We pick up the story in Luke 15:20, where we encounter the father's persistent, waiting love: "But while [the son] was still far off, his father saw him and was filled with compassion; he ran and put his arms around him and kissed him." We observe an anxious father, a father looking longingly down the road to see if his son might be coming home "on the next train." No matter how much shame that young man heaped upon his father's head in broad daylight, this father did not give up but persistently waited for his son to return home.

The father in Jesus' story evokes God the Father, who patiently waits and yearns and looks for the return of his children. Children like you and like me. Our Father, no matter what we have done, loves us enough to wait longingly for us.

OUR FATHER CELEBRATES

The reader of the parable of the prodigal son knows the persistent father threw a huge block party for his repentant, returning son. The father gave the son his ring, he gave him his robe, he gave him the best of his cattle, and he cooked up a feast.

Why? Because the Father who dances endlessly with the Son and the Spirit is the same Father who persistently yearns for us to join the dance. When we face this loving Father, when we enter into this divine dance, we encounter a God who throws a party of joy in celebration of those who enter back into fellowship with God.

So, when we pray, "Our Father who art in heaven," we are talking to a God whose love for us is persistent enough to wait for us to return home.

Facing this day:
Our heavenly Father waits for us to return home.

Scriptural focus:
*"But the father said to his slaves,
'Quickly, bring out a robe—the best one—and put
it on him; put a ring on his finger and sandals on
his feet. And get the fatted calf and kill it, and let us
eat and celebrate; for this son of mine was dead and
is alive again; he was lost and is found!' And they
began to celebrate."*
—Luke 15:22–24

Looking for God

*"The L*ORD* appeared to Abraham
by the oaks of Mamre,
as he sat at the entrance of his tent
in the heat of the day."*
—Genesis 18:1

I n the Midwest States, the expression "I'm from Missouri" does not usually come from someone informing us of where a person lives. Instead, this famous expression, straight from the heart of America's heartland folks, means, "I'm skeptical. Show me and I'll believe you." There is a Missourian in the heart of each of us—we often want to have proof for what we believe, proof even that God loves us.

I believe God honors the way we're made. Sometimes he packs up his bags, exits the heavenly palace, and comes to us in flesh and blood, as we are about to see in the story of Abraham and the angels.

LOOK FOR GOD IN OTHERS

I love the beginning of the story of God's visiting Abraham in the eighteenth chapter of Genesis. You can feel the narrative: Abraham was by the "oaks of Mamre" (wherever that was); Abraham was sitting "at the entrance of his tent" and it was "in the heat of the day." High noon, on the back porch, so hot even the birds are seeking shade—that graphic, that real.

Then God showed up.

However, Abraham thought that these were three human visitors, so he did what any host of this time would do—he honored ancient Near Eastern hospitality customs. He greeted his guests by bowing before them, giving them water, washing their feet, and offering them a shady place for some rest; and he got everyone in the household involved in preparing a feast. As they were eating together, the Bible narrative suddenly stops using the plural "they" for the three visitors who were visiting Abraham. At this point the author begins using "the Lord."

The three visitors were God.

Were they humans or were they angels? Abraham and Sarah thought they were humans. In these three humans Abraham and Sarah encountered God in flesh and blood. What they thought were human visitors to whom they showed hospitality was the presence of God.

Sometimes we see the face of God in others, and they are not always angels.

LOOK FOR GOD IN DISGUISE

Two men, Luke tells in the twenty-fourth chapter of his Gospel, were walking home to Emmaus from Jerusalem with their heads bowed low in depression after an intense Passover festival. They had hoped Jesus of Nazareth would bring peace to Jerusalem and send the Romans packing so they could worship God in freedom and holiness. They were explaining these things to a man walking with them. What they did not know was that this man, like the visitors to Abraham and Sarah, was God: the man they were walking with on the dusty road to Emmaus was Jesus himself.

Like Abraham, they invited their visitor into their home and offered him a meal. Somehow Jesus became the host and broke bread. When he did this, the men from Emmaus recognized that the one who had explained the whole Bible to them in such dramatic fashion was Jesus himself.

LOOK FOR GOD AT THE TABLE

Does your Missouri-heart need to be shown? If it does, come to the table—the table at the front of most churches, the table of communion.

From the days of Abraham to the days of Jesus, and from the days of Jesus until now, God moves into the neighborhood at the table. The table is *simple*: bread and wine, two ordinary foodstuffs. The table is *symbolic*: the bread is Jesus' body and the wine is Jesus' blood. The table is an *invitation*: you are invited to the table to feast on Jesus, to eat a small morsel of bread and sip some wine. At the table, God visits us.

Perhaps you'd like to see more. Maybe you'd prefer that God show up with some fireworks, or swoop down from heaven and heal everyone present, or suddenly turn everyone into an ecstatic frenzy so they would know God is present.

But not the God of the Bible, not the God who visits us and reveals himself to us in love. The God of the Bible shows up in ordinary ways, daily, in ordinary things for ordinary people.

If you want to be shown the face of God, come to the table, and you will see the God who gives himself for you and who invites you to feast on himself. There, in that small meal, you will find forgiveness, grace, mercy, power, and—most of all—fellowship with God and with one another. At the table we experience the love of God that put the Jesus Creed into motion.

Facing this day:
Come to the table and see God.

Scriptural focus:
"When he was at the table with them,
he took bread, blessed and broke it, and gave it
to them. Then their eyes were opened, and they
recognized him."
—Luke 24:30–31

God "On Call"

"Go home to your friends,
and tell them how much the Lord
has done for you,
and what mercy he has shown you."
—Mark 5:19

The dumbest thing I ever did in my life was drive an old junker of a car over 100 miles per hour on a two-lane highway. I wasn't thinking clearly enough—after all, I was a teenager—when I decided to test the limits of this car. Driving east on Highway 75 on my way to Dakota, Illinois, I cranked it up just to see if the car could do it. What I wasn't thinking of was that the road had some hills and some turns. As I looked at the speedometer and saw that I had crossed the magic line, I felt a rise in the car. I was slightly airborne because the road had crested slightly. More important—and I can see the sunlight and the colors to this day with unusual clarity—the road, which had very little shoulder, now began to turn, and I was inexperienced and stupid. I didn't mean to take my life in my own hands, but sometimes we don't know what we are getting into. Somehow, in the mercy of God and by applying the brakes and turning the car not too suddenly and keeping my wits about me, I managed to slow the car down and get my way through that turn.

I never again tried to get a car to 100 miles per hour.

God's mercy lurks in the shadows of your life. In the shadows of that day God's love came to me as mercy. I had done something stupid enough to kill myself. I cannot think of that day without whispering a brief prayer of gratitude to God for sparing my life, for showing me mercy.

GOD IS READY

"Mercy" is one of those words in the Bible that tells a story. Just as the only time the doctor comes to our home is when we are in need, the only time "mercy" shows up is when someone is in need. In the Bible, the one who doles out mercy is God, the God whose mercy gives direction to the Jesus Creed. God delights to be "on call" for mercy missions. Jesus, so it seems to me, was also on call in his earthly ministry, and that ministry visibly incarnated the mercy of God. Notice how the gospel writers talk about Jesus, because frequently their stories of Jesus are stories of mercy.

When he saw a man with leprosy—and of course Jesus knew the social implications of the ostracism and the labeling that the leper experienced—Mark tells us that Jesus was "moved with pity" (Mark 1:41). As Jesus went about proclaiming that the good news of the kingdom was now available to all, even the marginalized, and as he saw that the religious leaders did not care about the marginalized, Matthew tells us this about Jesus: "When he saw the crowds, he had compassion for them, because they were harassed and helpless, like sheep without a shepherd" (Matthew 9:36). Jesus embodies the attitude of God: God is ready to respond to those who are in need.

God's mercy lurks in the shadows of your life.

I don't know your shadows—perhaps you are struggling in a relationship or worrying about your children or sickened by the prospect of being laid off from your job. Or, perhaps you live in the shadows of something you've done wrong—maybe you've had an affair, maybe you've stolen something, maybe you've exploded in anger, maybe you've violated the trust of another.

Don't forget this: God's mercy lurks in your shadows, too.

WE NEED TO CALL GOD

God may be on call, but God awaits our calling. When the paralyzed man needed healing, he didn't sit at home moaning. When he heard about Jesus, he got together his friends and asked them to carry him to where Jesus was. So determined were these men—and we might think of the paralyzed man as a coxswain on a crew team calling out orders of where to go next—that they hauled the man to the top of a house, peeled away the roofing, and lowered the man before Jesus. When that man finally found himself resting before Jesus, perhaps covered with the grit of the roof, he was doing exactly what every person who needs mercy is capable of doing. He found himself facing Jesus because he knew Jesus was the face of mercy.

Face Jesus, for in that face we find the face of God's mercy, and the experience of God's mercy moves us out of the shadows of our own selves into the open light of loving God and loving others.

Facing this day:
Face Jesus today and you will find God's mercy.

Scriptural focus:
"As the eyes of servants look to the hand of their master, as the eyes of a maid to the hand of her mistress, so our eyes look to the LORD our God, until he has mercy upon us."
—Psalm 123:2

DAY 10

Promised Love

"The LORD, *the* LORD, *a God merciful and
gracious, slow to anger,
and abounding in steadfast love
and faithfulness, keeping steadfast love for the
thousandth generation, forgiving iniquity and
transgression and sin."*
—Exodus 34:6–7

O ne of the most gruesome scenes of the Bible
forms one of the greatest scenes in the Bible.
Old Abraham, tested more than any of us
would care to be tested, kept asking God for one thing—
a child for Sarah and himself. God kept promising to
Abraham that he would give them a son, but God and
Abraham were not on the same schedule. God had a
different sense of time and an odd sense of timing. One
day God scheduled a meeting with Abraham and showed
him the stars in the heavens and promised him then and
there that his descendants would be more numerous than
the stars in the sky. *A great promise,* Abraham must have
muttered to himself, *but we've got to start putting shiny
stars in our family sky.*

With Abraham pondering such thoughts, God put divine love on the line (and, as we will see, "in" a line).

AN UNUSUAL ACT . . .

God told Abraham—and here comes the gruesome part—to cut in half a heifer, a female goat, and a ram. Then God told Abraham to lay them opposite one another so they looked a bit like Rorschach inkblots. And he told him to lay a turtledove and a young pigeon opposite one another as well.

And then something unusual happened. To understand how unusual it is, we need to recall that this ceremony was the way the ancients entered into significant binding promises. If you wanted to make your promise to another deeply clear, you cut animals in half and then walked between them as a way of saying, "May this happen to me if I break my word." It was a deathly serious version of our legal contracts.

The greatness of this event followed next. Instead of God telling Abraham to walk through the labyrinth of promise to make sure Abraham assumed full responsibility for the promise, *God walked through the labyrinth of promise.* In fact, God put Abraham to sleep so that it became blatantly clear that God was doing all the promising here. Abraham simply got to watch and to accept God's unusual act. By walking between the animals, God was saying to Abraham, "I will do this to myself if I ever back down on my promise!" What appears to us as gruesome was normal for Abraham; what was great was how graphic God got in this act of promise.

God spoke in Abraham's day in Abraham's ways, and what God said was this: "My word is good. You can count on it."

. . . FOR AN UNUSUAL LOVE

What God implied by walking among the sacrificed animals was this: "I will be your God and you will be my people. I will always be here for you. If this relationship breaks down, you can know this: I am not responsible for the breakdown. I will remain faithful. My word is good. Watch me show you how seriously I take my promise to fill your sky with descendants."

God promised to take care of Abraham's family and God promised to take care of Abraham's personal welfare. Sometimes we think of God as "up there" or "off on a remote island." We think of prayer as ringing up God and hoping that he is not too busy taking other calls. Or we are a bit stunned to think that God could care about each of us down here on Planet Earth.

But God's message was clear to Abraham and his world: God put his love on the line for us by walking the line of commitment.

If God's commitment to us is a good word from God, so our commitment to God and our commitment to ourselves is to walk the same line God showed Abraham. Jesus urges us to love God and to love others, and many days we may wonder if we can manage the task. Some days we know we are not up to the challenge, and we know that if God's love is to flow from us, it must be a special work of God in us to pass God's love on. Instead of looking to ourselves or even at our own weaknesses, however, we are to look to the good word of God to empower us to remain faithful in the path God has walked for us—the path of loving God and loving others, the path of the Jesus Creed.

Facing this day:
God's promised love is as good as God's faithfulness.

Scriptural focus:
"He brought [Abraham] outside and said, 'Look toward heaven and count the stars, if you are able to count them.' Then he said to him, 'So shall your descendants be.' And he believed the LORD; and the LORD reckoned it to him as righteousness."
—Genesis 15:5–6

PART 3

The Jesus Creed and Its Loves

The Jesus Creed exhorts us to love others as ourselves. God loves us, and that love enables us to love ourselves with a proper self-love, to love those closest to us, to love those in God's family, and to love those who are needy.

Loving the Face in the Mirror

*"In everything do to others
as you would have them do to you;
for this is the law and the prophets."*
—Matthew 7:12

We might be a little surprised at what Jesus actually says in the Jesus Creed: Jesus taught that the standard for our love for others is our *self-love*. We learn to love others by extension from how we love ourselves. Like so many other lines in the Bible, no definition of "self-love" is offered. But, we can assume that self-love means caring for ourselves by feeding ourselves and clothing ourselves, seeking love by engaging in relationships with others, and loving God by following his commands and praying and worshiping. These sorts of endeavors frame how we learn to love others, and having a good sense of self-love is a sign of *shalom*, or peace, for Jesus.

Some people have a healthy self-image. As our daughter, Laura, matured into young adulthood, she would occasionally burst out a little note of joy with this line: "I love my life." Laura brought this sense of well-being to the surface when thinking about her life.

But you may not love yourself in a healthy way, and you may not even care for your life. So, let's begin today by taking a good look at the face in the mirror and learning to love who wears that face. There are good reasons for you to love you, for you to have a proper self-love.

LOVE YOURSELF BECAUSE OF WHO YOU ARE

Self-love, the kind of self-love Jesus assumed, emerges out of who we are.

The Bible's opening chapter tells us about the face in the mirror. We—all of us—are *eikons* of God—those made in "God's image." *All of us*. The good and bad of this world, the law-breaker and the law-follower, the tall and short and fat and skinny, the young and the old, the married and the unmarried, the wealthy and the poor, the sophisticated and the crude, the immigrant and the native . . . we could go on for pages. Love yourself because you are Godlike.

The psalmist knew this self-love when he said: "I praise you, for I am fearfully and wonderfully made. Wonderful are your works; that I know very well" (Psalm 139:14). Notice these words: we are "wonderfully" made, and all of God's works are "wonderful." Love yourself because you are wonderful.

We are God's *eikons*, "images of God," but the real *Eikon* of God is Jesus Christ. Paul tells us in Colossians 1:15 that Jesus is the "image of the invisible God." He also tells us that those who learn to face Jesus by taking away the veil of pretense will see Jesus, and gazing at Jesus transforms us into his *eikon* (2 Corinthians 3:18). If we are *eikons*, then we are made in the image of Christ. Love yourself because you are Christlike.

C.S. Lewis, in his *The Weight of Glory*, says, "It is a serious thing to live in a society of possible gods and goddesses, to remember that the dullest and most uninteresting person you can talk to may one day be a creature which, if you saw it now, you would be strongly tempted to worship." And because of this weight of glory, there "are no ordinary people."

Self-love emerges from knowing that we are Godlike and Christlike. Even more, a proper self-love emerges from loving God and loving Christ and extending that love to ourselves.

LOVE YOURSELF BY FORGIVING YOURSELF

Each of us messes up, each of us does things wrong, and each of us sins. The good news of the Bible is that God doesn't leave us in the messes we make. God forgives. When Adam and Eve messed up, God sought them out to restore them and repair the relationship. Jesus forgave people over and over in his day. At the heart of the message of the gospel is this simple truth: God's love reaches us in an act of gracious forgiveness for what we have done.

But sometimes even as we confess that God forgives us, we hang onto our guilt and our shame and our former alienation. Today, claim and act on this promise: Since God has forgiven you of your sins, you can accept that forgiveness by following God's own path of forgiveness by forgiving yourself for what you have done. Go ahead. Open up the door, let God see your messes, and let God take them away—and clap for God as you see him export them right out the door.

They're gone.

Love yourself by letting God take your sins away and forgiving yourself as God has forgiven you.

LOVE YOURSELF BY DOING

The Golden Rule teaches that we are to "*do* to others as you would have them *do* to you." The assumption is that we know how to do for ourselves what we would like done for ourselves. The Jesus Creed and the Golden Rule permit a proper self-love, the self-love that knows we are God's *eikons* and that we are being conformed to the *eikon* of Christ. This proper self-love both flows from God and flows back into God. True self-love, then, is to know ourselves as God knows us and to treat ourselves as God treats us. True self-love, as Jesus teaches us, leads to love of others.

Here is something you can *do* for yourself today. Open your Bible to Psalm 139 (printed below) and ponder your way through it, asking God to reveal what true self-love is.

1   O Lord, you have searched me and known me.
2   You know when I sit down and when I rise up;
       you discern my thoughts from far away.
3   You search out my path and my lying down,
       and are acquainted with all my ways.
4   Even before a word is on my tongue,
       O Lord, you know it completely.
5   You hem me in, behind and before,
       and lay your hand upon me.
6   Such knowledge is too wonderful for me;
       it is so high that I cannot attain it.

7   Where can I go from your spirit?
       Or where can I flee from your presence?
8   If I ascend to heaven, you are there;
       if I make my bed in Sheol, you are there.

⁹   If I take the wings of the morning
         and settle at the farthest limits of the sea,
¹⁰   even there your hand shall lead me,
         and your right hand shall hold me fast.
¹¹   If I say, "Surely the darkness shall cover me,
         and the light around me become night,"
¹²   even the darkness is not dark to you;
         the night is as bright as the day,
         for darkness is as light to you.

¹³   For it was you who formed my inward parts;
         you knit me together in my mother's womb.
¹⁴   I praise you, for I am fearfully and wonderfully
         made.
         Wonderful are your works;
         that I know very well.
¹⁵   My frame was not hidden from you,
     when I was being made in secret,
         intricately woven in the depths of the earth.
¹⁶   Your eyes beheld my unformed substance.
     In your book were written
         all the days that were formed for me,
         when none of them as yet existed.
¹⁷   How weighty to me are your thoughts, O God!
         How vast is the sum of them!
¹⁸   I try to count them—they are more than the sand;
         I come to the end—I am still with you.

19   O that you would kill the wicked, O God,
        and that the bloodthirsty would depart from
        me—
20   those who speak of you maliciously,
        and lift themselves up against you for evil!
21   Do I not hate those who hate you, O LORD?
        And do I not loathe those who rise up against
        you?
22   I hate them with perfect hatred;
        I count them my enemies.
23   Search me, O God, and know my heart;
        test me and know my thoughts.
24   See if there is any wicked way in me,
        and lead me in the way everlasting.

Facing this day:
You are wonderfully made. Love yourself as
someone God made to love and be loved.

Scriptural focus:
*"The second [commandment] is this, 'You shall love
your neighbor as yourself.'"*
—Mark 12:31

DAY 12

The Jesus Creed
Begins at Home

*"He who loves his wife
loves himself."*
—Ephesians 5:28

Loving God and loving others begins at home, because the home is the workshop of love. Those who abide in the Jesus Creed are loved by God and love God in response; but God's love creates the kind of self-love that prompts each of us to love others, including those in our own family or who are closest to us.

Paul's statement—"he who loves his wife, loves himself"—contains a subtle point that many skip over. To say that the husband who loves his wife in fact loves himself is a variation on the Jesus Creed applied to family life. Just as Jesus said to love your neighbor "as yourself," so Paul observes that a husband who loves his wife does so *because he loves himself*. One of the foundations for family love and family life is a proper self-love.

The Jesus Creed life participates in a cycle: It begins
with God's perfect love in the communion of the Father,
Son and Spirit; it explodes into the creation of you and
me as *eikons*; it comes to fruition in proper self-love; it
manifests itself in love for those who love others who
love God; and the cycle begins all over again. Family love
participates in this cycle.

LOVE YOURSELF FOR YOUR FAMILY'S SAKE

Many husbands and fathers don't love their wives or
their children because they don't love themselves. The
same is true of many wives and mothers and children
and siblings. Family love begins with learning to love
yourself. Let's remind ourselves of what we said in the
previous chapter: we are *eikons* of God. God loves us,
and that means we are set free to love ourselves—for how
can we love God if we don't love what God loves?

We can forgive ourselves and remind ourselves that we
are becoming "Christlike." If God's love is perfected in
his love for the Son, and if we are "in" that Son, then
God's perfect love for his Son is directed squarely at us
because we are "in Christ." Even if you don't feel you are
worthy of God's love, the Son is—and that means, since
you are "in Christ," the Father loves you as the Father
showers his love on the Son!

So, today, *because you are a family member,* love yourself. So, today, *for the good of your spouse, your family, and those closest to you,* love yourself in that perichoretic dance of God's love.

LOVE THAT SPECIAL PERSON AS YOURSELF

Not everyone is married or still married. But, everyone has special persons or a special person in his or her life. I believe these words of Paul about husbands loving wives can be extended to exhort us to love as ourselves those we specially love, whether that special person is a spouse, a family member, or a friend. As you care for yourself, as you look after yourself, as you dream for your own life, so care for, look after, and dream for that person. The Jesus Creed, if it is to take root at all in our life, begins right here—with a spouse, with family members, and with special friends; and it spreads from our closest relationships into all the rest of our relationships.

Perhaps we need to be reminded of the needs of the elderly—of aging parents or siblings or neighbors or the seniors in our community or church. Many of them are incapable of getting out of the home by themselves or of traveling or even of doing chores so many of us take for granted—like grocery shopping or attending a local public event. We can love these people as ourselves too.

If you listen to the persons who are special to you and observe them, you will learn what makes them tick, what they most like, and what God has made them to be. Now you can commit yourself in God's power, with patience and only with their cooperation, to love those persons as yourself.

LOVE CHILDREN AS YOURSELF

For those of us who are parents, the Jesus Creed shapes our love for our children. Parenting finds its way to extremes: some parents are neglectful and rationalize their neglect in the name of "developing the independence of their children." Others are "helicopter parents," who hover over every need of each child and nearly suffocate them with attention. Somewhere in between those two extremes is a Jesus Creed kind of love for your children: as we do not neglect ourselves and as we should not suffocate ourselves with too much attention, so we need to find the proper balance of loving our children as ourselves.

Not everyone is married, and not everyone married has children, but each of us is called to follow Jesus in showing special love and attention to children. As he let the children find their way to him, so we can let them find their way to us. How? Perhaps we can serve at church or in summer camp, or in our neighborhood where children have special needs. More and more churches are developing day care ministries as they sense the needs of the parents in their communities.

Most of us can give examples, but here are two from our family. Two colleagues in my department at North Park have young children. Brad and Barb Nassif have Melanie, and Joel and Karla Willitts have Mary and Zion. They are not our children, but we care about the children of our friends. Once, Kris saw something in a store and said, "Melanie would love this." So she bought it and wrapped it up and gave it to Melanie as a small gift. When the Willitts' twins finally came home—they were in the hospital almost two months—Kris and I volunteered to watch them for a morning so Karla could sleep and Joel could get some work done.

The Jesus Creed begins with love of family and those closest to us.

_____

Facing this day:
A Jesus Creed day begins when you start it off by loving your family as yourself.

Scriptural focus:
"I am my beloved's and my beloved is mine."
—Song of Songs 6:3

Love God's People

"And [Jesus] replied,
'Who are my mother and my brothers?'
And looking at those who sat around him,
he said,
'Here are my mother and my brothers!
Whoever does the will of God is my brother
and sister and mother.' "
—Mark 3:33–35

Good titles capture not only ideas but also the mood of the day. Perhaps no title captures a dominant mood in the American church better than Dan Kimball's *They Like Jesus But Not the Church*. After hours of sitting in coffee shops talking to ordinary people about Jesus and Christianity, Dan discovered the following reasons people don't like the church: because the church is an organized religion with a political agenda, it is judgmental, it oppresses females, it is homophobic, it is arrogant about other religions, and it is led by fundamentalists who take the Bible far too literally.

I teach students who fit into this mood of liking Jesus but not the church. But, I fear this mood is out of sync with the Jesus they claim to like, because the Jesus of the Bible is the one who gave himself for the church. Jesus comes with the church, and the church comes with Jesus. It is, after all, his bride! The church has its faults, some of them worse than others, but this is hardly a discovery. The irony of this newly published critique is that the Jesus who attracts us is the one who overtly claims that he invites imperfect people to his table. If we expect the church to house only perfect people, perhaps we've come to the wrong table! Put differently, perhaps our problem is that we love our *idea* of the church and what it *ought* to be rather than the *reality* of the church and what it is.

Now, lest I be misunderstood, let's not forget that Jesus summons us to his table so we can be transformed into people who love God and love others. Let us also not forget that the church is a hospital for sinners, not a haven for the already perfect.

LOVE THE FAMILY OF GOD BECAUSE
IT ENCIRCLES JESUS

I love the image of Jesus in the middle of a circle made up of his followers and friends and family and probably some religious seekers. Mark tells us in Mark 3:34 that

Jesus looked at those who "sat around him." Earlier in that context, some family members had come down from Nazareth to Capernaum to find him. To do so, they had to "knock on the door." Some of those at the home informed Jesus that his family was at the door, and Jesus—rather abruptly as we read the passage—declared that his *real* family was already sitting in a circle around him. The dim element of this story is that his family members thought, as Mark 3:21 tells us, that Jesus had "gone out of his mind," and they had come to rescue him from himself.

Jesus' own family members were like those in Dan Kimball's book—they wanted Jesus, but they didn't want him associating with all those sinners sitting in that circle around him. Their problem with Jesus was not that his followers weren't good enough. No, their problem seems to be that they thought Jesus was too good for those who wanted to be attached to Jesus. Jesus had created a hospital for sinners, and his family members preferred a place for the perfected. His family members soon learned to enter that circle and sit with the others, but, like us, they had their critical days.

We love the church because Jesus is in the middle of the church. Because Jesus is encircled by people who need his teachings and his life-changing graces that flow from his life, death, and resurrection. Because he is surrounded by those who love him. We can love the church today because, whether the church is "doing church" well or not, it witnesses to what we think is the roundabout at the heart of the city of God: Jesus himself. Instead of despising the church because of its weaknesses, perhaps we should learn to love the church *because it welcomes the weak and offers healing over time by simply gathering around Jesus.*

LOVE THE FAMILY OF GOD BY PARTICIPATION

Paul's image for the church in chapters twelve through fourteen of his first letter to the Corinthians is a body—with each body part representing the various gifts each person brings to the coordination of the body. One of Paul's most potent statements is found in chapter twelve, verse seven: "To each is given the manifestation of the Spirit for the common good." To "each" of us—to you and to me and to everyone who comes to the table. To each is "given the manifestation of the Spirit"—to each is given a gift that somehow manifests God's Spirit. And to each is given a gift "for the common good." We are not given gifts to hoard for ourselves or so our pantry will be filled for every possible emergency. We are gifted by God—and here we are back again to the Jesus Creed's second element of loving our neighbor as ourselves—"for the common good." God gives us gifts so we will give them to others.

Jesus is at the center of the family of God, and that means love is present. Smack dab in the middle of Paul's exhortation for Christians to participate in that church, Paul stops to tell us about loving others (1 Corinthians 13). Why? The only way to participate in the church with sanity is to realize that God's love and Jesus' love empower us to love others—whether they are "out of their mind" or not!

Facing this day:
We can love Jesus' family as a hospital for the wounded and not a haven for the perfected.

Scriptural focus:
"So then, whenever we have an opportunity, let us work for the good of all, and especially for those of the family of faith."
—Galatians 6:10

DAY 14

Love the Needy

"If a brother or sister is naked and
lacks daily food,
and one of you says to them,
'Go in peace; keep warm and eat your fill,'
and yet you do not supply their bodily needs,
what is the good of that?
So faith by itself, if it has no works, is dead."
—James, brother of Jesus (James 2:15–17)

L oving others includes, but is not limited to, the
needy. It begins in God's own love within the
Trinity, explodes into the creation of *eikons* who
are shaped by God to love God, self, and others, and this
cycle of love begins with those closest to us, and ripples
into our community of faith and then into anyone we
might meet who is in need.

Who, today, is your neighbor in need? When the scribe,
trying to justify himself, in the tenth chapter of Luke

asked Jesus, "Who is my neighbor?" Jesus answered that question by revealing that a neighbor is *anyone in need*.

The world's top ten list of the most needy people today would include those infected with AIDS, those suffering in Darfur, the homeless, tsunami victims, Katrina victims, Iraqi children, orphans in Romania, boat people, refugees, and famine victims. Too many others could be added. Most readers of this book are not next-door neighbors of these deeply needy people. Many of us write checks monthly or annually for relief of these needy people. But such compassionate work does not complete our responsibility.

Are we missing our own needy? Are we hearing the cries of our neighbors? Do we know about the needs of ordinary people around us who are crying out because of collapsing marriages, difficult children, financial crises, loneliness, despair, work relationships, career disappointments?

Open your windows for the sounds of the needy, and open your eyes to see the pain of the needy. We need to become sensitive to the needy who are next to us, who are on the path in the trip from our own Jerusalem to our own Jericho. Most of the needy who surround us don't wear signs with the words "I am needy." Instead, we have to find them—and they are everywhere.

LISTEN WITH THE EARS OF JESUS

How to begin? Listen with the ears of Jesus.

Jesus hears with the ears of mercy and readiness to help. When someone told the synagogue ruler Jairus that his daughter was dead, Jesus *overheard* the statement and said, "Do not fear. Only believe, and she will be saved" (Luke 8:50). When Lazarus's sisters were grieved, Jesus *overheard* them and said, "This illness does not lead to death" (John 11:4). When the centurion expressed amazing faith because he loved his servant so much, Jesus *heard* right through his words to his deepest heart and "[Jesus] was amazed." Jesus then rang that man's bell of honor in front of everyone with this statement: "Truly I tell you, in no one in Israel have I found such faith" (Matthew 8:10). And when Jesus *heard* that some religious zealots had kicked a healed man out of their synagogue, Jesus chased him down to lead him to worship the one true God (John 9:35–37).

Jesus heard the cries of others because he was listening. Are we listening with his ears? NorthBridge Church, in a community near us, approached the local school board and asked this question: "How can we help you?" They were informed of a pressing and expensive need—a building that didn't meet code—and NorthBridge bundled up its energy and funds and got that building up to code with their own labor and funds because they listened with the ears of Jesus.

LOOK WITH THE EYES OF JESUS

How to begin? Look with the eyes of Jesus.

Jesus saw with the eyes of faith, hope, and charity. When he *saw* four fishermen, he saw not four scruffy men but four pastors (Matthew 4:18, 21). When he *saw* the crowds, he saw the hungry (5:1). When he *saw* Peter's mother-in-law in pain, he saw her need, not as an interruption in his otherwise scheduled day but as an opportunity to help (8:14). When he *saw* men lowering a sick person through a roof, he saw not aggressive men but men of faith (9:2). When he *saw* Matthew at a tax booth, he saw not a Roman collaborator but a potential apostle (9:9).

Jesus looked through the obvious to see a need and then acted to meet that need. Are we looking with the eyes of Jesus?

LINK WITH THE HANDS OF JESUS

How to begin? Link with the hands of Jesus.

Jesus has the hands of healing, renewal, life, and restoration. When Jesus saw the unclean leper, he *touched* him with the hand of healing (Matthew 8:3). When his disciples were dizzied by an encounter with God and shaken with fear, Jesus *touched* them with the hand of renewal (17:7). When he saw the young man lying dead on a funeral bier and saw the man's mother in grief, Jesus *touched* the bier with the hand of life (Luke 7:14). When one of the disciples reacted to Jesus' arrest by chopping off the ear of a man, Jesus *touched* the man with hand of restoration (22:51).

Jesus touched those in need with hands of grace. How might we touch others with the hands of Jesus?

Facing this day:
Listen with the ears of Jesus, look with the eyes of Jesus, and touch others with the hands of Jesus.

Scriptural focus:
"For I was hungry and you gave me food, I was thirsty and you gave me something to drink, I was a stranger and you welcomed me, I was naked and you gave me clothing, I was sick and you took care of me, I was in prison and you visited me."
—Matthew 25:35–36

PART 4

The Jesus Creed Becomes the Sermon on the Mount

If the Jesus Creed is the most famous of Jesus' statements, the Sermon on the Mount is Jesus' most famous sermon. In this section, we explore how the Sermon on the Mount illustrates the central elements of the Jesus Creed: loving God and loving others.

DAY 15

Loving All Kinds

"Blessed are the poor."
—Matthew 5:3

When some read the Sermon on the Mount all they can think of is the word "demand" and its noisy chaser "obedience." But if Jesus teaches us that the essence of all of God's demands and the face of all our obedience is loving God and loving others—the Jesus Creed as taught in Mark 12:28–32—then even the Sermon on the Mount expresses a discipleship fired by love for God and love for others. Those who love God and others, in other words, live a life not unlike that outlined by Jesus in the Sermon on the Mount.

The Beatitudes, if we read them properly, push us to love God and to love others. What the Beatitudes reveal is that we are to embrace the surprises among God's people and that we are to love all those who love God.

LOVE THOSE WHO LOVE GOD

I love to get to church early and watch God's people find their seats. Since we attend a very large church, I get to see lots of people. If it weren't for familiarity, we would be surprised by who comes to church, who loves God, and who gathers with us to worship God and to read the Bible and to sing with us.

Jesus, as it were, sat at the back of his little gathering of followers and began telling everyone that there are lots of little surprises in God's kingdom. Instead of being a gathering of just one kind of person—righteous, God-fearing, Torah-minded males—Jesus' tattered kingdom included those who came hoping for a handout, those who were depressed by death and destruction, those whom everybody considered nobodies, those for whom life was all about doing what was right, those who saw needs in the eyes of others, those whose hearts thumped with crystal-clear goodness, those whose war was to get warring groups back together again, and those who sat at Jesus' table but were battered and bruised because they followed Jesus. Some read the Beatitudes as Jesus' version of what Paul calls the "fruit of the Spirit," where Paul speaks of love and joy and peace and self-control (Galatians 5:22–23). This is not what the Beatitudes are. Instead, they are a listing of the sorts of people who have found their way into the kingdom vision of Jesus, the sorts of people who love Jesus.

All kinds of people love God. We can embrace this diversity.

LOVE THOSE WHO LOVE OTHERS

Christians don't always do what they should, and we hear many sharp critics pointing out our faults, but when Christians follow Jesus well, they put on an amazing display of love and compassion and caring.

I am proud of the activism of our students. At North Park University, where I teach, some have rallied student support at the national level and have tirelessly worked with local leaders to make more folks aware of the problem of homelessness. (Did you know that the average homeless person in the United States is nine years old? A student told me this in my office.) Our students routinely minister to the homeless in Chicago, and they "sleep out" one night a year to express solidarity with those who suffer. In the city of Chicago, loving others easily leads to loving the homeless. Not everyone is called to a personal ministry to the homeless, but one local expression of the Jesus Creed is to love those who extend mercy to those in need.

Jesus loved those who loved others and called them out for their good work. He blessed—as strong a "call out" as you can have in the Jewish world—those who wept for others, those who showed mercy to those in need, and those who worked for peace in their local contexts. What I am suggesting here is that those who are blessed by Jesus are those who are engaged in loving others—he is blessing those who are living the Jesus Creed.

LET'S NOT JUST TALK ABOUT LOVE

Not only can we embrace the diversity of the church of those who follow the Jesus Creed, but also we can join that diversity by joining hands with those who love others.

What are you "known for"? For what would Jesus give you a shout-out? We are always tempted to give shout-outs to those who give themselves for the suffering in Darfur and for those who minister to AIDS victims in Africa. To be sure, we can each do our part for the most needy in our world, but each of us is called to see those in need around us. We begin at home and in our neighborhood and extend our neighborhood to anyone we meet. Are we responding to those we see who are needy?

Do so and you will hear as from a distance that little word of Jesus: "Blessed are you."

Facing this day:
Embrace the diversity of those who respond to the needs of others in the name of God.

Scriptural focus:
"Blessed are the merciful, for they will receive mercy."
—Matthew 5:7

DAY 16

This Little Light of Mine

"You are the salt of the earth."
"You are the light of the world."
—Matthew 5:13, 14

Of whom do you think when the expression "influence others for Jesus" comes to mind? Would it be St. Augustine, whose famous *Confessions* have led countless Christians to find their life by journaling? Would it be St. Macrina, who propped up the ministries of Eastern Christians in prayer and good works? Would it be St. Benedict, whose *Rule* has given structure to the lives of myriads of Christians? Would it be St. Francis or St. Clare, whose very lives remind everyone that life is more than what we possess? Is it one of the Reformers, or a great writer, or your pastor, or your friend? Who has been that "influence for Jesus" for you? Are you carrying on that person's influence to others? Jesus Creed love influences others in the way of Jesus.

Jesus spoke of this influence his followers were to have, casting before his listeners two images—salt and light.

We find these two images in the opening chapter of the Sermon on the Mount. But what do these images suggest? Each one suggests several ideas. Salt flavors and purifies and preserves; light dispels darkness and gives us light for our feet. Read the entire passage, and we can observe that by the end of Jesus' statements, it is quite clear what Jesus has in mind: "[L]et your light shine before others, so that they may see your *good works* and give glory to your Father in heaven" (5:16).

The influence we are to have on others by living the Jesus Creed comes through good works. We are called by Jesus to be people of good works—to love others by doing them good. We can do good by providing meals and visiting the sick, and giving comfort to the depressed, and remembering the special days on other people's calendars, and inviting them to our home.

SHARE THE LABOR OF GOOD WORKS

When Jesus said, "*You* are the salt of the earth" that "you" is plural. All of his disciples were to be salty and enlightening, and that meant he was summoning each of his followers to be persons of influence through good works. What Jesus had in mind was the kinds of concrete good works in our community that Jesus Creed followers accomplish.

Here's something to remember: it is not up to you alone and it is not up to me alone to accomplish these good works. It is up to *all of us together*. Each of us can be influential, but the plan is for each of us to contribute to the kingdom group of Jesus so that the group has the influence of good works. It is the image of a church doing well or a choir performing or a class shaping, rather than that of an individual Christian soaring to the heavens or a soloist showing off or a disciple knowing more than anyone else. When each does his or her part, we become— as a group—the influence *we* are designed to be. The Jesus Creed is meant to be lived out together with others.

GUARD YOUR GOOD WORKS

Jesus warned his followers about salt becoming insipid and about candles being buried under a basket. Why? He knew influence, once lost, is hard to recover. Whether we think of fallen pastors or lapsed Christians, each of us knows how difficult it is to regain broken integrity. This is a warning we all need to hear. But there's good news as well.

The fallen and the lapsed can regain their influence. Think of Peter—the Number One Apostle who turned his back on Jesus when it mattered most for Jesus to have support. But Jesus had some strong and merciful words with Peter, found in the Gospel of John's last chapter, that brought Peter back into the sphere of influence.

So where do we begin? Instead of pointing fingers at the fallen and lapsed, we can take steps to guard our good works. How? By offering ourselves to God, by prayer, by moral vigilance, and by staying in fellowship with others who can keep us on the path. We can commit ourselves today to be persons who guard our good works. To love others in the way of the Jesus Creed is to help others to stay on the path, and it is to trust others to help us stay on the path.

LET YOUR GOOD WORKS LEAD TO GOD

Many today are concerned about doing good works solely so we can have an opportunity to tell others about Jesus. Others worry about being too aggressive in evangelism. So, how can we steer between these two poles and still let our good works lead to God?

We begin with *behavior*—doing good things for others. Next we check our *motive*: good deeds need to be propped up by doing good for the sake of the other and for the sake of God. We also have *confidence*: our prayer is that our good works will somehow be used by God to show his goodness. Finally, sometimes there is *opportunity*: people of the Jesus Creed wait for God to prompt someone to ask the question, "Why are you doing this?"

Facing this day:
Influence others in the way of the Jesus Creed.

Scriptural focus:
*"Religion that is pure and undefiled before God,
the Father, is this: to care for orphans and widows
in their distress, and to keep oneself unstained by
the world."*
—James 1:27

True Greatness

"Whoever does [these commandments]
and teaches them will be called great
in the kingdom of heaven."
—Matthew 5:19b

Good deeds turn ordinary people into great people. But in a culture that is addicted to celebrity, that swoons at the sight of the rich, and that is shaped by the opinions of the powerful, it is hard for all of us to adjust our thinking to the way the Jesus Creed works. The Sermon on the Mount expresses the Jesus Creed with concrete illustrations of the kind of person Jesus considered great. The Jesus Creed ethic counters everything our culture considers great.

Let's reverse conventional wisdom, which calls attention to celebrities for doing good. Let's try to reframe the ruling story of our world and suggest that true greatness is measured, not by fame and fortune, but by goodness and mercy. We can all applaud the work of household names who are working intensively to eliminate AIDS and poverty, such as Bono and Rick Warren. We know about their good deeds because they are considered "great" in our culture. But you, too, can become great even if no one ever learns your name, even if you never make the headlines of the local newspaper, and even if no one ever writes your biography. For Jesus, *anyone who practices his teachings is a great person.* Let's work hard to shed the connection of greatness with celebrity, and create a new sense of what makes someone great.

Good deeds, because they are Jesus Creed acts of love for others, turn ordinary people into great people. This is what Jesus means when he says, "but whoever does [my commandments] and teaches them will be called *great* in the kingdom of heaven" (Matthew 5:19). Jesus revises our image of greatness in Matthew 5:21–37 with four illustrations in a row that reveal the heart of the Sermon on the Mount. The term "great," one might say, describes those who love God and others well.

YOU ARE GREAT IF YOU HAVE GOOD RELATIONSHIPS

Great people keep reconciled relationships at the top of their list of "Today's To Do's." So important are relationships to Jesus that he commands his followers to work through their anger as quickly as possible and to avoid any kind of insult, put-down, or slander. Even if they are at the temple in Jerusalem, Jesus says, and they remember they are out of sorts with someone, they should—he's exaggerating to good effect—drop their temple sacrifice, find that person, and make peace.

We don't often think about it this way, but maintaining peaceful, loving relations with those we know is what makes a person great. Many of us might admit it is easier to be a celebrity than to be great in terms of the Jesus Creed.

YOU ARE GREAT IF YOU REMAIN FAITHFUL IN MARRIAGE

Jesus valued marriage as a lifelong commitment (Matthew 5:27–32). Saying to Jesus, "Since I'm not divorced, I'm faithful," is not enough. Husbands and wives can avoid the divorce court and have an awful, Jesus Creed–denying relationship. No, avoiding divorce court is not enough. Jesus measures faithfulness differently: faithfulness is something in the mind and heart (not lusting after others, not envying someone else's spouse) as well as in the law court (not divorcing).

Jesus knows that God shaped wives and husbands, not just to stay together, but also to love one another in the kind of faithful commitment to one another that God has repeatedly shown to us. That kind of loving, faithful commitment is a sign of greatness.

YOU ARE GREAT IF YOU TELL THE TRUTH

To show just how significant loving-others relationships were to greatness, in the Sermon on the Mount Jesus summons his followers to practice steadfast honesty. Here's what Jesus teaches: "Let your word be 'Yes, Yes' or 'No, No'" (Matthew 5:37). Honest words are simple words. They are unadorned, without cosmetics, genuine words straight from the heart and mind.

Once our family was invited to the home of an Amish couple, Milton and Lizzy Yoder, in Middlebury, Indiana. As we were knocking on the door, they pulled up to the home in their horse-drawn buggy. Lizzy welcomed us into her home as Milt "parked" the buggy and took care of the horse. After we sat ourselves down on simple (hard) chairs in a simple room, Lizzy asked us if we would like a glass of water, which we gladly accepted. Not soda pop. Not coffee. Just water. Simple, plain water from simple, plain people in a simple, plain family.

That's how Jesus wants our words to be—simple, clear, truthful. Nothing added, no need to flavor them up with oaths or buckle them up tightly with special words of emphasis like *really, really* to give our words more honesty. When you always tell the truth, your words need no buttresses to support their honesty. Truth-tellers are great people.

YOU ARE GREAT IF YOU AVOID REVENGE

Jesus' fourth point is about revenge. Everyone is wounded at some point, and pursuing a more just world is a good thing. But thirsting after revenge and settling scores and seeking to humiliate or put someone in his or her place are signs of "little people." Great people, Jesus says, create a cycle of grace instead of vindication. They accomplish this by doing good to those who have done them harm. For Jesus, great people turn the other cheek, give an extra cloak, and go the second mile because they live the Jesus Creed that is shaped by loving others as ourselves.

Facing this day:
Greatness is measured by loving relationships, not by fame and fortune.

Scriptural focus:
"First be reconciled to your brother or sister."
—Matthew 5:24

Loving Wrongdoers

"But love your enemies."
—Luke 6:35

I n the Sermon on the Mount, Jesus urges his followers
to love their enemies. Now, enemy-love is a wondrous
principle to pronounce, but it is a demanding love to
live. Still, for Jesus, enemy-love is not a romantic ideal
but the rugged reality of the Jesus Creed. First, we must
have enemies in order to have enemy-love, and to have
enemies we need the memory of having been wronged
by someone. Only because of wounds and memory does
the enemy-love of the Jesus Creed get summoned into
action.

Yale theologian Miroslav Volf, a Yugoslavian Christian,
endured compulsory military service. He was tested and
persecuted and mentally tortured because of his faith.
He recounts his excruciating experience in his book
*The End of Memory: Remembering Rightly in a Violent
World.* The maturing question he has had to live with is
a question many of us also need to ask: "How should the
one who loves," who lives by the Jesus Creed, "remember

the wrongdoer and the wrongdoing?" Loving the enemy often begins in the mind and in our memory.

Perhaps it is far too easy for us to assign enemy status only to those at unreachable distances and whose enemy status reaches enormity—Osama bin Laden, Saddam Hussein, Adolf Hitler, and Joseph Stalin. It is far too easy to cough up the thoroughly romantic claim that we should love them. In Jesus' world, such an enemy status was assigned to Rome, but the enemy Jesus has in mind is much closer to home than unreachable tyrants like Tiberius sitting in far-off countries on thrones of iron. The enemy, our enemy, is the one who has wounded us; enemy-love seeks to heal those wounds.

Loving the enemy is the only way to stop the cycle of violence, the only way to accomplish justice and then to move beyond it. The Jesus Creed love of enemy-love is the only way to create a kingdom reality on earth.

ENEMY-LOVE BEGINS IN OUR MEMORY

Loving our enemy begins in the mind with our memory, and it is a hard memory to travel. Remembering that we have been wronged leads us to two options. We can choose to stew in our memories of the wrong and enjoy a feast of condemnation, the feast that never satisfies, and we can choose to dwell in this stew of condemnation. Sadly, if we do, we let the wrongdoer define us.

Or, in the grace of God, we can let the cross of Jesus Christ—where the Innocent One was mortally wounded but who nonetheless offered grace through that mortal wound—define us and our relationship with those who have wounded us. First, we offer the wounds, and the one who wounded us, to the cross by condemning the wrongdoing. Enemy-love doesn't casually dismiss the wrongdoer or the wrongdoing; it condemns the wrong.

In God's grace, enemy-love then remembers not only the wrong and the wound but also that God has absorbed all wounds in order to turn them around into grace. Once we face God's gracious reversal of wounds, we seek the grace of reconciliation by remembering that, in spite of our own wrongdoing, God loved and forgave us. In that work of God, we turn our memory of wounds into the hope of grace, and we offer that grace to those who have wounded us. In offering the grace that genuinely acknowledges wrongdoing, we unleash God's cycle of grace by offering grace to others.

We need a cross-shaped memory to practice the enemy-love of the Jesus Creed. At the cross, not only did God forgive us but also he established the cycle of enemy-love. Jesus said, "Father, forgive them; for they do not know what they are doing" (Luke 23:34). As Volf expresses his own experience, "The memory of the Passion urges . . . me to place the memory of suffered wrong in the service of reconciliation."

ENEMY-LOVE WELCOMES THE
HUMANITY OF THE ENEMY

What is hard for us to admit about the enemy is that in the face of the enemy, we see an *eikon* of God, someone made in God's image, and therefore we see the face of Christ—who is the perfect *Eikon* of God. Instead of shrinking the other person to the size of our personal villain, we need the eyes of Christ to see in the other person, in spite of the wrongs they have done, someone whom God loves, someone for whom Christ has died, and someone with whom we journey in this life. It is hard to see an abuser or an oppressor or a criminal as an *eikon* of God, but that is how the Jesus Creed fleshes itself out in calling us to enemy-love.

Enemy-love somehow finds a way both to admit that the offender is an *eikon* of God—a cracked one to be sure—and someone we are to welcome to the table of *eikons* because God made that *eikon*. This does not mean we wipe away the wrongs or dismiss the deeds until they have been seen for what they are. But it does mean that we are called as practitioners of the Jesus Creed to welcome the humanity of the enemy.

"This fellow," the experts said of Jesus, "welcomes sinners and eats with them" (Luke 15:2). Will we join Jesus at the table?

ENEMY-LOVE BECOMES PRAYER AND BLESSING FOR OUR ENEMY

As Jesus says in his great Sermon, "bless those who curse you, pray for those who abuse you" (Luke 6:28). If our memories need to become cross-shaped, so also do our blessings and prayers. It takes the courage of faith, faith in the kind of God who forgives at the cross, to lift in prayer those who have wounded us. It takes faith to extend God's blessing to them. Perhaps the greatest prayer we can pray for those who have wounded us is the simple one: "Lord, work in this person to become the person you want them to be." Maybe we can go no farther. That far we can go.

Pope John Paul II extended forgiveness to the man who shot him, Mehmet Ali Agca, and Miroslav Volf mentally forgave the captain who tortured him. They did this by remembering the cross, welcoming the humanity of the offender, and extending grace through prayer and blessing to the other.

Facing this day:
The Jesus Creed summons us to
love even our enemy.

Scriptural focus:
"Father, forgive them."
—Luke 23:34

Spiritual Disciplines
as Love

*"Beware of practicing your piety before others
in order to be seen by them;
for then you have no reward from
your Father in heaven."*
—Matthew 6:1

Spiritual disciplines are the new fashion for Christians. Many Christians speak of their practices of fasting, solitude, contemplation, Bible reading, silence, meditation, aid for the poor, and journaling. Each of these is good and important. Each can also be easily diverted from its true end. The Sermon on the Mount contains a principled approach to spiritual disciplines: the principle is found in Matthew 6:1 (quoted above), and three illustrations of disciplines—almsgiving, prayer, and fasting—reveal the genius of the principle (6:2–18).

We can practice spiritual disciplines for three different ends: We can do them in order to convince ourselves that we are pious, we can do them to gain the approval of others, or we can practice them in order to love God and others more. They can be self-absorbing and other-affirming, or they can be God-pleasing. God designs spiritual disciplines to increase our love for him and for others. Spiritual disciplines that do not result in living the Jesus Creed are done for unworthy ends.

I was stopped in my tracks one day when studying a book by John Ortberg called *The Life You've Always Wanted,* a book on the spiritual disciplines. "The true indicator," he observes, "of spiritual well-being is growth in the ability to love God and people. *If we can do this without the practice of any particular spiritual disciplines, then we should by all means skip them.*" Yes, I said to myself as I recovered from what is rarely said by anyone, that's the point. We are not asked by God to practice these disciplines in order to convince ourselves of our own spirituality—"I fast, therefore I am spiritual." We don't do these to show others we are pious—"I practice solitude, therefore I stand above the ruck of others." No, we are asked to exercise the disciplines in order to become those who put into practice the Jesus Creed of loving God and loving others. If we've mastered loving God and loving others (which we haven't done), we don't need the disciplines. But, since we haven't mastered the Jesus Creed, we need the disciplines—as long as we do them for the right ends. Here are three ways to convert spiritual disciplines into Jesus Creed disciplines:

GIVE OF YOUR BOUNTY AS AN ACT OF LOVE OF GOD AND OTHERS

Humans don't need to be tempted to vanity in order to give. Vanity over our spirituality runs so deep in the human soul, sometimes in the subtlest of ways, that the last thing we need is the assurance that our name will appear in the Sunday bulletin or on a brick if we make a donation. Jesus encouraged his followers to *work at secrecy when it came to almsgiving.* Thus, he says in the Sermon on the Mount, "But when you give alms, do not let your left hand know what your right hand is doing" (Matthew 6:3).

What we learn is that the more secretive we become about our giving, the more we can focus on God. Which is the whole point. Our "tithes and offerings" are our gifts to God for what God has done, what God is doing, and what God will do. As you give, convert your giving into an act of loving devotion to God.

PRAY AS AN EXPRESSION OF YOUR
LOVE FOR GOD AND OTHERS

Another of the spiritual disciplines is prayer, and the Lord's Prayer remains essential for defining prayer and for the discipline of prayer. The Lord's Prayer has two parts—the God part and the "us" part. The first part expresses what prayer looks like when we love God; the second part expresses what prayer looks like when we love others. When we love God, we desire God's name to be held in high reverence; we yearn for God's kingdom to come, and we long for God's will to be done. When we love others, we pray for their daily needs to be realized, we ask God for a cycle of forgiveness to be unleashed for them, and we request of God for each of us to be spared from falling into sin. As we pray to God and for others, perhaps today we can envision prayer as an act of love.

FAST IN ORDER TO LOVE GOD AND
PROVIDE FOR OTHERS

The third discipline Jesus mentions here is fasting. Fasting is to deny the body food because the moment is too sacred to indulge in physical pleasure. Because it requires such discipline to be a great faster, it is easy for the one fasting to think he or she has done something special. Perhaps such persons expect God to bend the divine will to their own wants or for others to give them special attention. Jesus warned his followers about the desire for congratulations about fasting. He was standing firm on biblical teachings.

All we need to recall are the searing words of Isaiah 58:6–7: "Is not this the fast that I choose: to loose the bonds of injustice, to undo the thongs of the yoke, to let the oppressed go free, and to break every yoke? Is it not to share your bread with the hungry, and bring the homeless poor into your house; when you see the naked, to cover them, and not to hide yourself from your own kin?"

Fasting, if done properly, leads us to love others.

———————

Facing this day:
Practice spiritual disciplines as gifts from God to lead you to love God and others.

Scriptural focus:
"He has told you, O mortal, what is good; and what does the Lord *require of you but to do justice, and to love kindness, and to walk humbly with your God?"*
—Micah 6:8

DAY 20

At the Center of a Centered Life

"But strive first for the kingdom of God and his righteousness, and all these things will be given to you as well."
—Matthew 6:33

S tatistics have proven repeatedly that we have more leisure time than any generation in history. Those statistics reveal that Americans on average enjoy nearly forty hours per week of leisure time. But Americans, somehow, manage to convert leisure time into busy time, because being busy is one way we measure who is important. Yet busyness scatters our inner life. "We are rush freaks," Al Gini tells us in his splendid book *The Importance of Being Lazy*. Abraham Lincoln once said something that might jostle us into thinking anew about what matters most in life: "My father taught me to work, but not to love it. I never did like to work, and I don't deny it. I'd rather read, tell stories, crack jokes, talk, laugh—anything but work."

Our obsession with work and busyness, and Abe Lincoln's homey reminder, both lead us to a question: If we could choose the absolute center of our life, what would it be? Would it be work? Would it be hanging out? Would it be what Jesus urges us to put at the center? Jesus knew that center point, and he showed us the way to it: at the center of a centered life is God and God's way.

THINGS NOT AT THE CENTER

In the Sermon on the Mount, Jesus pointed out four things that are not found at the center of a life that loves God and loves others: food, drink, clothing, and tomorrow. "Therefore I tell you," Jesus said, "do not worry about your life, what you will eat or what you will drink, or about your body, what you will wear. Is not life more than food, and the body more than clothing?" (Matthew 6:25). Each of us struggles with vital and even important concerns that shove and push their way to the center, even when those are not to be at the center. For some it is *food*—eating too much or spending too much money on food; for others it is *drink*—drinking too much of the wrong libation; for yet others it is clothing—

spending too much time caring for our appearance and not enough on the inner life.

Something else not found at the center of the centered life is tomorrow. "So do not worry about tomorrow," Jesus says in one of his most potent statements, "for tomorrow will bring worries of its own. Today's trouble is enough for today" (Matthew 6:34).

CENTER ON THE KINGDOM

At the center of a centered life is God and God's way—the kingdom of God. This is why Jesus said, "But strive first for the kingdom of God" (Matthew 6:33). In speaking of the kingdom, Jesus wants his followers to live now as if we find ourselves in a society in which the will of God is already established. To make the kingdom central is to live by faith.

The insight for you and me today is that God's work in this world is bigger than what God is doing in you and me. If at the center of the centered life is God's kingdom, then we can devote ourselves to God only by devoting ourselves to God's people and to bringing about what God wants for our world. Giving ourselves up for what God is doing in this world is the only way to discover ourselves in the center of God's world and the only way of finding our way to the centered life.

CENTER ON RIGHTEOUSNESS

Jesus said: "But strive first for the kingdom of God *and his righteousness*" (Matthew 6:33). The word "righteousness" was a favorite word among Jews of Jesus' day: it was ascribed to people, such as Jesus' earthly father (Matthew 1:19), who knew the Torah and observed the Torah. To call someone "righteous" in that day was like calling someone a "saint" in ours. For one of Jesus' followers, to seek righteousness is both to know and to put into practice the teachings of Jesus. Because God is at the center of a centered life, the ways of God expressed in the teachings of Jesus are also at that center. We can make this center a living part of our lives by centering on God and God's ways—the kingdom and righteousness.

Jesus' promise is that those who find their way to that center will have all they need—and even more than that.

Facing this day:
Center on God and God's ways.

Scriptural focus:
"For where your treasure is, there your heart will be also."
—Matthew 6:21

Principles to Live By

"In everything do to others
as you would have them do to you;
for this is the law and the prophets."
—Matthew 7:12

A fine moment in the history of translating the Bible was when J.B. Phillips translated Romans 12:1–2 like this: "Don't let the world around you squeeze you into its own mould, but let God re-mould your minds from within." We might call these two graphically translated verses from Romans a principle for a good life. But principles of life are easier to state than to live effectively. If this was one of Paul's great principles, what were the principles of Jesus?

Jesus' fundamental principle of life was the Jesus Creed, the summons to love God and to love others. The Sermon on the Mount converts the Jesus Creed into more concrete examples of how to put into practice the kingdom vision of Jesus. The Sermon is full of concrete principles, and we will look at four of them from Matthew's seventh chapter.

KNOW YOURSELF FIRST

How many times have you heard this word of Jesus as a warning not to be judgmental? "Do not judge, so that you may not be judged" (Matthew 7:1). Nine of ten young adults who are outsiders to the Christian faith think Christians are too judgmental, and over half of young Christians agree with our critics. Only one of five outsiders thinks the church is a loving environment, and more than half of churchgoers agree with our critics. (Oddly enough, more than three-quarters of pastors think their church is a loving environment instead of a judgmental one.) Christians obviously have some work to do, but the way to do this is not to suspend judgment but rather to learn how to be more Jesus Creed–like in moral discernment.

But do you think the conventional use of this principle of Jesus is wise? Are we never to render judgments about the morals of others? Perhaps it is wiser to observe that there is a difference between the words *judgment* and *discernment*. Judgmental people find the weaknesses of everyone, prop themselves up into self-righteousness by comparing themselves—always favorably—to others, and, sadly, often drive themselves to become depressed cynics. The one who chomps away on others eats his own soul.

Jesus summons his followers to a different way, to a way of loving discernment: *Before you say anything about someone*, Jesus teaches, *first think of yourself.* This question by Jesus creates a new way of life: "Why do you see the speck in your neighbor's eye, but do not notice the log in your own eye?" (Matthew 7:3). A good look at the mirror of our own soul reveals that we don't have everything together, and this self-knowledge creates a pattern of empathy and sympathy for others. With this penetrating question, Jesus shows us that judgmentalism needs to give way to empathic, loving discernment.

TREAT GOD'S WAYS WITH REVERENCE

A second principle is found in these words: "Do not give what is holy to dogs; and do not throw your pearls before swine" (Matthew 7:6). Here Jesus reminds us to treat what is sacred with the utmost reverence, a principle our culture needs more than ever. I confess that I appreciate how many Christians in traditions other than my own genuflect or kneel before the communion table or cross themselves when the Trinity is mentioned. Why? Because such behaviors reveal that one knows one is in a sacred place among sacred things summoning us to sacred behaviors.

Jesus himself and Jesus' gospel, the sacred pearls of the Christian's life, are also sacred. There are times, Jesus expresses in this principle, when it is unwise to speak of Jesus, to correct someone, or bring up the subject of God or the gospel. Why? Because those in the audience will take cheap shots at what you value most. The time will come when you will find such people more receptive, and that is the time when the sacred can become more public.

TRUSTING THE GOOD GOD

Ask, seek, knock, Jesus said in a third principle. Why? Because God is good. If we humans, who are sometimes good and sometimes not, give good things to those who ask, "how much more will your Father in heaven give good things to those who ask him!" (Matthew 7:11).

Recently a woman wrote to me out of despair. She was in a rough patch health-wise, and one of her trusted friends led her to see that her ill health had opened up some old emotional wounds that were also in need of healing, some family wounds of rejection. She asked us to pray for her and informed us that she was living by faith, telling herself every moment of the day: "Mom left me,

God doesn't leave me. Mom couldn't love me, God loves me. Mom rejected me, God doesn't reject me." Becky's story is what it means to live by faith in difficult times by trusting that God is a good God even when our own lifeboat doesn't seem buoyant.

LIVE BY THE GOLDEN RULE

I used to think the Golden Rule was pablum, food for a child. I also thought that when I grew up spiritually, I'd put away pablum and eat meat. The older I get, the more experience I have in the church and with Christians, and the longer I seek to follow the Jesus Creed as developed in the Sermon on the Mount, the more the Golden Rule looks like the real meat and the supposed deep things look like commentary on the Golden Rule.

Here is our challenge from Jesus' fourth principle: try living by the Golden Rule. Try it the way Jesus summoned us: "In everything." Not just with those you love and like, or with your favorite neighbors and friends. Live the Golden Rule with everyone. Not just on Sunday or in the evening when you get home, or on weekends when you have free time, but always: when you get up and when you go to work and when you are at work (yes, here, too) and when you are in a scrap with someone and when you are stressed.

Treating others as you would like to be treated, which is the second half of the Jesus Creed and the essence of the Golden Rule, is a principled legacy that creates a different kind of life. Completely different.

Facing this day:
Those who live by Jesus' principles
live a different kind of life.

Scriptural focus:
"Everyone then who hears these words of mine and acts on them will be like a wise man who built his house on rock. The rain fell, the floods came, and the winds blew and beat on that house, but it did not fall, because it had been founded on rock."
—Matthew 7:24–25

PART 5

The Early Christian Leaders Teach the Jesus Creed

The Jesus Creed had a profound impact on three of the most dynamic leaders in the earliest churches. In this part we will look at how the Jesus Creed shaped the moral teachings of the apostle Paul, James the brother of Jesus, and the apostle John.

DAY 22

Spiritual Freedom

"For freedom Christ has set us free."
—Galatians 5:1

The apostle Paul, whose letters reveal the most profound theology of the first generation of Christians, discovered that freedom formed the center of the Christian life. In the middle of some serious theological situations about faith, works, and circumcision, Paul paused to exhort the churches at Galatia to learn how to treat one another. The banner Paul wanted hanging outside all of his churches was one word: "Freedom!" Here's Paul's central exhortation to the Galatian Christians: "For freedom Christ has set us free."

But what is freedom? Some think of freedom as *personal*, the freedom to do whatever they please. But that version of freedom contrasts with everything Jesus and Paul taught. Others think of freedom in *political* terms—the government's role is to provide us the opportunity to pursue happiness, and the government's role is to protect our rights. But political freedom is far from Jesus' and Paul's minds.

So, what does a Christian sense of freedom mean? It means finding Jesus Christ and learning to experience liberty from sin and its shackles so we can live a life of loving God and others. Humans are truly free only when they love God, love themselves, and love others. Freedom flows directly from the Jesus Creed. So, how can we find this freedom?

LIVE IN THE SPIRIT AND YOU WILL FIND FREEDOM

At the bottom of all of Christian reflection on the Christian life is the rock-solid conviction that God's Spirit animates everything we are to do. The Jesus Creed life requires the *ruach* of God's *Ruach*—the wind of God's Spirit. So, first, we need to slow down, to quiet our hearts and our minds. Then we must turn our face toward God, asking God to do with us what God did to the early Christians at Pentecost: to breathe the Spirit on us. Don't expect this to be an ecstatic experience. Expect only that God will honor what God most wants to do: give his life to us so we can live his kind of life.

Paul promised his readers two blessings of the Spirit. The first blessing of the Spirit is that there is a way out of the web of fleshly habits, a way that leads us to discover freedom from sin; the second is that we are therefore liberated from the accusations of the Law. "Live by the Spirit, I say, and do not gratify the desires of the flesh," and "if you are led by the Spirit, you are not subject to the law" (Galatians 5:16, 18). Each of us has fleshly habits, and many of us have done our level best striving to undo them. Discipline has its place, but discipline is not the power that changes life. The power to change comes from the Spirit. Therefore, Paul's words exhort us to open ourselves to the renewing graces of the Spirit.

LOVE OTHERS AND YOU WILL FIND FREEDOM

The Jesus Creed teaches that life is about loving God and loving others. Paul was a rabbi, one who knew the Torah very well. But what he had to learn was that the Torah needed to be understood as a Torah of the Jesus Creed. Notice these radical words of Paul's: "For the whole law is summed up in a single commandment, 'You shall love your neighbor as yourself'" (Galatians 5:14). Amazingly, rabbi Paul was willing to reduce the *whole* Torah down to one command, the second half of the Jesus Creed: "love your neighbor as yourself." Paul did not come upon this insight himself. He heard it from those who had heard Jesus. Rabbi Paul became a Jesus Creed Paul, empowered because he learned that the ability to love your neighbor as yourself entered into the community only through God's Spirit of freedom.

God grants us the freedom to do what God made us to do. What God made us to do was to love others. Anytime we use the freedom to harm or dishonor others, we deny ourselves true freedom. And anytime we use our freedom to love others, we find ourselves truly free.

Many people are in a quest for inner freedom. But, when we seek freedom in order to consume it ourselves— for example, saying, "I want to be able to do whatever I want to do"—we enslave ourselves to our ego. But, when we love others as ourselves, not only do we discover the joy of love but also we find we are free at last.

———

Facing this day:
The Jesus Creed leads us to freedom in God's Spirit.

Scriptural focus:
"For you were called to freedom, brothers and sisters; only do not use your freedom as an opportunity for self-indulgence, but through love become slaves to one another."
—Galatians 5:13

Our Debt of Love

"Owe no one anything,
except to love one another;
for the one who loves another has
fulfilled the law."
—Romans 13:8

Those who live the Jesus Creed have one moral debt: the debt to love others. Normally the word *debt* leads us to think about money and our mortgage. But Paul urges us to think what those who live the Jesus Creed *owe* others. What is our debt to one another?

Paul's words about our common moral debt, quoted above, were one more application of the Jesus Creed for the Christians in Rome. Yet, today's Western culture is shaped by two lesser moral "debts": toleration and political correctness. The two work together. In our tolerant society, we have agreed not to use labels for one another that are potentially harmful. But, to make the Jesus Creed a living part of our lives involves more than tolerating someone—which translates to "putting up with" in a condescending manner. The exhortation of the Jesus Creed to love is something other than to tolerate; instead, it calls us to engage, to become friends, to serve the other, and to join hands with that person. And love is more than avoiding labels, because love removes those labels to form a society of friendship and fellowship.

Paul learned that some Christians at Rome were labeling themselves "the strong" and others as "the weak." Involved was the difficulty the latter had with eating "unclean" foods like pork or not celebrating Sabbath according to the Jewish tradition. Paul responded to this situation, once again, with the Jesus Creed to point the way toward the moral debt of love.

OUR DEBT OF LOVE DOES NOT WRONG THE OTHER

I like Paul's subtle variation on a portion of the Jesus Creed. After summing up the commandments with the words "Love your neighbor as yourself," Paul wrote that "love does no wrong to a neighbor" (Romans 13:9–10). The wording here is general because his vision is global: love simply doesn't do another person wrong. The way to create a loving society that transcends labeling one another is to begin with this principle of Paul's.

There are two sides to the debt of love. First, there is the side of active *engagement*: we act for the good of the other—spending time with others, helping them with chores, asking about their lives, or praying for them. Second, there is the side of active *avoidance*: we avoid doing things that will wound or wrong or harm that person. The more we know a person, the more we know what to avoid and what not to do. (In many cases, the person is likely to let us know!)

OUR DEBT OF LOVE DOES NOT JUDGE

When necessary, Paul did not shy away from strong words in admonishing his churches: "Why do you pass judgment on your brother or sister? Or you, why do you despise your brother or sister? For we will all stand before the judgment seat of God" (Romans 14:10). Jesus Creed love doesn't label, it doesn't condescend, it doesn't exclude as unworthy, and it doesn't act judgmentally.

There is a fine line between judgment and discernment. Paul got it right in this passage. He clearly discerned that there are "the strong" and there are "the weak," though calling someone "weak" is normally not a compliment. Yet Paul's discernment broke down judgmentalism. Notice Paul's loving discernment: "Some judge one day to be better than another, while others judge all days to be alike. Let all be fully convinced in their own minds. Those who observe the day, observe it in honor of the Lord. Also those who eat, eat in honor of the Lord, since they give thanks to God; while those who abstain, abstain in honor of the Lord and give thanks to God" (Romans 14:5–6).

OUR DEBT OF LOVE LOOKS OUT FOR THE OTHER

Within the church, many have been the battles over the meaning of Romans 14:13: "Let us therefore no longer pass judgment on one another, but resolve instead never to put a stumbling block or hindrance in the way of another." What, after all, is a "stumbling block" or a "hindrance"? Am I captive to the conscience of another? We might ask whether if one Christian in my church finds offense in my drinking a glass of wine, I am obligated to do what she prefers.

To be sure, these are the practical questions. Once again, it is a matter of discernment. But it is a matter of discernment *in community*. And this is Paul's point: Christians look out for one another to avoid leading one another down dark paths to sin. It is not that we have to agree with one another on everything—the passage from Romans 14:5–6 makes that clear. It is rather that we guard our behaviors to make sure they don't lead another off the path into dangerous bogs.

We have seen that the Jesus Creed isn't simply a motivational poster by Jesus that can be tacked to our bedroom wall to remind us in the morning that we are to love God and others. The Jesus Creed, in the hands of this great apostle and in the hands of the church for us, has become the moral foundation for how Christians can live with others to demonstrate the kingdom of God.

———————

Facing this day:
The first debt to pay is to love others.

Scriptural focus:
"For the kingdom of God is not food and drink but righteousness and peace and joy in the Holy Spirit."
—Romans 14:17

Memory Love

*"You do well if you really fulfill the royal law
according to the scripture, 'You shall love your
neighbor as yourself.' "*
—James 2:8

Love grounded in memory reaches out to others. James, regarded by tradition to be the brother of Jesus, learned the value of the Jesus Creed from his older brother (Jesus). When James was pastor of an early Jewish-Christian church, traditionally thought to be in Jerusalem, he saw something that brought the Jesus Creed to life. This group of followers of Jesus was meeting in what appears to be a synagogue (James 2:2). In that most public of places, James watched followers of Jesus kowtow to the rich by giving them prominent seats, and he saw the same followers of Jesus humiliate the poor by asking them to find a spot on the floor.

It made no sense to treat the poor this way. Why? Memory. Simple memory. James asked his congregation to remember their past and to let their own memory shape love.

LOOK FOR THOSE WHO HAVE FALLEN
THROUGH THE CRACKS

Most of the earliest followers of Jesus were the poor who had fallen through the cracks of society. Jesus' mother was poor, and Mary's own words in the Magnificat reveal her condition (Luke 1:46–55). Jesus began his most famous sermon with the words "Blessed are you who are poor" (Luke 6:20). After Pentecost, the first community of Christians in Jerusalem creatively helped the poor (Acts 2:42–47). The apostle Paul beat down doors asking for aid to help the poor (Galatians 2:10). The experienced memory of the earliest churches was the reality of poverty.

Somehow, though, the earliest Christians in Jerusalem forgot their own economic condition. Instead of supporting one another, they turned against one another to favor the rich. What was most needed was someone with clear-headed memory. James was that person. Here was his question for his fellow poor brothers and sisters: "Has not God chosen the poor in the world to be rich in faith and to be heirs of the kingdom that he has promised to those who love him?" (James 2:5). "Well, yes, he has," is the only response the Christians in Jerusalem could have mustered in what had to be an embarrassing moment of memory.

Are there those who have fallen through the cracks in your church or in your neighborhood or in your community? Let us use our collective memory. We know what the church has been through, so we can use our memory to awaken in us sensitivity to those around us. Perhaps we need to look at events in our own churches that assume access to funds that unintentionally exclude the poor; perhaps our stories and life experiences cannot be shared by those with less income. If we live in the affluent Christian West, our memory anchors us in a story of anything but abundance.

LOVE THE BROKEN

As James, brother of Jesus, learned to put the Jesus Creed into practice, he developed a special sensitivity for one group very close to home. James remembered his family. Notice his words: "Religion that is pure and undefiled before God, the Father, is this: to care for *orphans* and *widows* in their distress, and to keep oneself unstained by the world" (1:27). James had not forgotten his past. Some traditions inform us that Joseph died and left Mary a widow—with five sons and some daughters (Mark 6:3). James remembered what it was like for his mother to be widowed and what it was like to be an orphan. In that world, to be without a father (or a mother) was to become an "orphan." In our world "orphan" means "without parents," but in James' world it meant losing either of one's parents.

James drew upon his memory and it gave him a ministry.

Each of us has a past of experiences that have shaped us. Many of us, truth be told, seek to escape those experiences. Some from poor backgrounds seek to live on Wall Street in order to escape the memory of hardship. Some of us were neglected children, and we might be tempted never to bring another child into this world in order to shut out our pain. James counsels another way. Instead of escaping our past, James urges us to *remember our experiences for the benefit of others.*

Perhaps your memories are mostly good. Perhaps you are experienced in a supportive family, a caring church community, a friendly neighborhood. . . . It doesn't matter, because each of us can convert our memories into a ministry of loving our neighbor as ourselves.

———————

Facing this day:
Convert your memory into a ministry.

Scriptural focus:
"Listen, my beloved brothers and sisters. Has not God chosen the poor in the world to be rich in faith and to be heirs of the kingdom that he has promised to those who love him?"
—James 2:5

Footwashing Love

"So if I, your Lord and Teacher,
have washed your feet,
you also ought to wash one another's feet.
—John 13:14

P aul and James clearly were learning to put the Jesus Creed into practice in the daily realities of the early churches. The apostle John, who watched Jesus wash feet, tells the story of that event, and in so doing, he exhorts us to do the same for others. Now, most of us don't literally wash one another's feet, so let me simply relate the story of Dawn Husnick, whose story illustrates what the apostle John remembered about how Jesus himself practiced his own Jesus Creed—his command to wash the feet of one another.

After some tough years with alcohol, failed personal relationships, and depression, Dawn found her feet for the journey. She now works part-time at a hospital emergency room in the Chicagoland area as she and her husband prepare to serve in China.

In my years in the ER, I saw Jesus daily doing His Kingdom work in and through a group of His followers. It was a true expression of the church. One day stands out beyond all the others and left me radically changed forever. It was the day I saw Jesus face to face.

"Dawn . . . can you lock down room 15?" yelled out my charge nurse as I crawled up to the nurse's station. Two security guards stood outside the room, biceps flexing like bouncers anticipating a drunken brawl. My eyes rolled as I walked past them into the room to set up. The last lock clicked into place as the masked medics arrived with [Name, N.] strapped and restrained to their cart. The hallway cleared with heads turned away in disgust at the smell surrounding them. They entered the room and I could see N. with his feet hung over the edge of the cart covered with plastic bags tightly taped around the ankles. The smell was overpowering as they uncovered his swollen, mold-encrusted feet. After tucking him in and taking his vital signs, I left the room to tend to my other 10 patients-a-waiting.

Returning to the nurse's station, I overheard the other Nurses and Techs arguing over who would take N. as their patient. In addition to the usual lab work and tests . . . the doctor had ordered a "shower" complete with Betadine foot-scrub, antibiotic ointment and non-adherent wraps. The charge nurse looked in my direction, "Dawn, will

*you please take N.? Please? You don't have to do the nasty foot-scrub. Just give him the sponge in the shower."
I agreed and made my way to gather the supplies and waited for the security guard to open up the hazmat shower.*

As I waited with N., the numbness of my business was interrupted by an overwhelming sadness. I watched N . . . restless and mumbling incoherently to himself through his burley scruff of a beard and 'stache. His eyes were hidden behind his ratted curly shoulder length mane. This poor shell of a man had no one to love him. I wondered about his past and what happened to bring him to this hopelessly empty place? No one in the ER that day really looked at him and no one wanted to touch him. They wanted to ignore him and his broken life. But as much as I tried . . . I could not. I was drawn to him. The smirking security guards helped me walk him to the shower as bits and crumbles of life on the street fell in a trail behind us.

As we entered the shower room I set out the shampoo, soaps and towels like it was a 5 star hotel. I felt in my heart that for at least 10 minutes, this forgotten man would be treated as a king. I thought for those 10 minutes he would see the love of Jesus. I set down the foot sponge and decided that I would do the gentle Betadine foot-scrub by myself as soon as his shower was finished. I called the stock room for two large basins and a chair. When N.

was finished in the shower I pulled back the curtain and walked him to the "throne" of warmed blankets and the two basins set on the floor beside.

As I knelt at his feet, my heart broke and stomach turned as I gently picked up his swollen rotted feet. Most of his nails were black and curled over the top of his toes. The skin was rough, broken and oozing pus. Tears streamed down my face while my gloved hands tenderly sponged the brown soap over his wounded feet. The room was quiet as the once mocking security guards started to help by handing me towels. As I patted the last foot dry, I looked up and for the first time N.'s eyes locked into mine. For that moment he was alert, aware and weeping as he quietly said, "Thank you." In that moment, I was the one seeing Jesus. He was there all along, right where he said he would be.

Dawn's story visibly reminds us that we, whether we are asked literally to wash the feet of someone in need or not, are asked to put the Jesus Creed into practice by serving one another. Our example is Jesus, and our memoried symbols are the basin and the towel.

Facing this day:
Jesus is our example of footwashing love.

Scriptural focus:
"'Lord, when was it that we saw you hungry and gave you food, or thirsty and gave you something to drink? And when was it that we saw you a stranger and welcomed you, or naked and gave you clothing? And when was it that we saw you sick or in prison and visited you?' And the king will answer them, 'Truly I tell you, just as you did it to one of the least of these who are members of my family, you did it to me.'"
—Matthew 25:37–40

The First Move of Love

"Whoever does not love does not know God,
for God is love."
—1 John 4:8

The apostle John, known as the apostle of love, creatively adapted the Jesus Creed to the churches he pastored that were at one another's throats. So, instead of a love-God and love-others form of the Jesus Creed, John pressed home the importance of loving those in the community of faith. He wrote: "The commandment we have from [Jesus] is this: those who love God must love *their brothers and sisters* also" (1 John 4:21). Inside the walls of the church, the Jesus Creed becomes unflinching love for one's fellow travelers in the way of Jesus.

This is not always easy. Sometimes it is easier to love those far away than those near and (not always so) dear. Sometimes familiarity breeds contempt, and because this happens so often, the apostle John steps in and says, "Friends, the Jesus Creed challenges us to love those we know up close and personally *in spite of what we know*

*about those people and in spite of our checkered history
with them.*"

John points us to the path of loving those we know
best, and he deepens the ground out of which the Jesus
Creed life grows. John teaches that we participate in God
when we learn to love one another.

BECAUSE GOD IS LOVE, WE ARE TO LOVE

When John writes his well-known "God is love"
statement, he does not mean to say that love itself is
God. Were John to be saying "love is God," he would
be depersonalizing God and making God little more than
an abstract principle. Rather, God, who is Person, is love
because love is what happens among the persons of the
Trinity. Anyone who claims to walk in this life with God
walks on the path of love.

John couldn't be any clearer about the nature of love:
"Whoever does not love does not know God, for God
is love" (1 John 4:8) and "We love because [God] first
loved us" (4:19). God's love is supremely manifest in
Jesus Christ, as John asserts when he writes: "God's love
was revealed among us in this way: God sent his only Son
into the world so that we might live through him" (4:9).

We are to love even our rascally Christian comrades
because we lay claim to know God—the God who is

love. When we think of the odd collection of folks in our community of faith, perhaps we need to remind ourselves not to focus on the faults in others—for that will turn our love off—but to look at the supremely sacrificial love of God—and that will turn our love back on.

LOVE IS A CYCLE

Our history with one another can create a cycle of un-love. To undo the cycle of un-love and to reanimate the cycle of love, the follower of the Jesus Creed looks to God's love for us: "Beloved, since God loved us so much, we also ought to love one another" (4:11). Cycles of un-love find their way systemically into the fabric even of church life.

Phillip Yancey, in his marvelous book *What's So Amazing about Grace?* tells his own story of falling into the cycle of racism. That systemic cycle of un-love only came to end when both African American and White American Christians were willing to stop the cycle, sit at table with one another, express their wounds and fears, listen to one another, and enter into a new commitment to love one another.

Only by seeing the supreme example of love in God's love for us are we empowered to end the cycles of un-love in our communities. Who will make the first move? We need only to look to God, who made that first move.

God's cycle of love can continue as we learn to participate in God's first move.

LOVE IS ACTION

As John reminds us, "Little children, let us love, not in word or speech, but in truth and action" (1 John 3:18). We are sometimes tempted to reduce love to indescribable emotion suddenly emerging in our breast and weakening our knees. This emotion makes our hands break into a cold sweat and keeps us awake at night. Those fresh chemical responses in our body can't be denied, but love is more than that. Love, John says, is "truth and action." Or we might say "active truth" or even "truth in action."

"To say that God is love," Frederick Buechner tells us, "is either the last straw or the ultimate truth." This ultimate truth invites you and me to walk with God, the God who makes that first move to end cycles of un-love.

Facing this day:
Join God in ending the cycles of un-love.

Scriptural focus:
"For this is the message you have heard from the beginning, that we should love one another."
—1 John 3:11

Resourceful Love

"Above all,
maintain constant love for one another,
for love covers a multitude of sins."
—1 Peter 4:8

The apostle Peter also practiced the Jesus Creed. He grew up reciting the *Shema* daily, and he was there when Jesus amended the *Shema* into the Jesus Creed by adding "love your neighbor as yourself" to that standard Jewish reminder to love God. And Peter learned to live by Jesus' new creed and learned to be resourceful about letting it find its way into his life and pastoral work. So, when Peter wrote his first letter to the churches in his care, love was at the top of his list. "*Above all,*" he wrote to them, "maintain constant love for one another" (4:8). At the top of the list, first and foremost, here's where it all begins: love for one another.

Love, because it is at the top of the list, becomes resourceful—the way children can make cardboard boxes into an afternoon of fun, or a mechanic can convert a tool or two into all he needs, or a cook can turn chicken into any ethnic taste you might want, or a committed couple can find their way through a rough patch. Those committed in the long term to one another know that love is resourceful. The resource begins in God's love for us in Jesus Christ. Love makes tinkerers of all of us.

LOVE THE INVISIBLE JESUS

The silent part of the Jesus Creed is the first part, the part that commands us to love God with every globule of our being. Rarely does anyone in the early church remind us that our task is to love God or to love Jesus. Peter is one of those rare exceptions as he writes: "Although you have not seen him, you love him; and even though you do not see him now, you believe in him and rejoice with an indescribable and glorious joy" (1 Peter 1:8). Peter was impressed with his churches' love for Jesus *although* they had not seen him. Peter also knew that love for the "invisible" Jesus unleashed the way of love in the community. He knew God's love for us in Christ was also God's gift of love to us.

Most Christians learn to love Jesus in one way: they read the Gospels in order to receive this gift called Jesus. When we read the Gospels, we encounter Jesus by watching his actions, listening to his words, and learning to walk with him at our side. But over time we learn another way: we learn to follow the "invisible Jesus" who reveals in the daily grind of our life that love finds a way.

LOVE THE VISIBLE HUMAN

It is sometimes easier to love the "invisible" Jesus than the visible human at our side—our spouse or our family members or our friends or our neighbors or those into whom we bump as we walk this life. Peter knows how hard it is to love others: "Now that you have purified your souls by your obedience to the truth so that you have genuine mutual love, love one another *deeply* from the heart" (1 Peter 1:22). First, we receive the gift: the gift of God's love to us in conversion and baptism. Next, we receive the challenge: love one another "deeply"—or, as a more literal rendering of *ektenos* would have it, "strenuously." The word suggests a deliberate, constant effort to let love find a way, the way runners stretch themselves to accomplish their goal and receive the prize.

Love shouldn't become overly romanticized. Love is hard work at times, especially when it involves stretched and strained relationships. But, if we let love do its work, love is resourceful enough to find a way into our visible relationships.

LOVE OTHERS SO MUCH YOU COVER WRONGS

When love becomes the kingpin, Peter tells us it will do its work of miracle-making, because love has the ability to get beyond wrongs. "Above all," Peter writes, "maintain constant love for one another, for love covers a multitude of sins" (4:8). As Karen Jobes says so well, the love that covers sins "does not let wrongs done within the Christian community come to their fullest and most virulent expression." This covering-of-wrongs-love shows us why Peter uses the word *ektene*, "strenuously," again. Love stretches us, but it also stretches itself over the wrongs and faults of others. Instead of accusing, resourceful love sees and understands, sees and forgives, sees and stays with, and because it does all these things, it gets beyond the wrongs to a life that engulfs our faults in a forgiving, healing, embracing grace.

Facing this day:
Love finds a way.

Scriptural focus:
"Finally, all of you, have unity of spirit, sympathy, love for one another, a tender heart, and a humble mind."
—1 Peter 3:8

Boundary-breaking Love

*Peter: "God has shown me
that I should not call anyone profane or
unclean."*
—Acts 10:28

The biggest challenge for the earliest followers of Jesus such as Peter, beyond embracing the cross as God's plan of demonstrating love, was embracing Gentiles as brothers and sisters (in Christ). But the love of the Jesus Creed crosses boundaries. The first major breakthrough came one day when Peter and a Roman military leader named Cornelius had simultaneous visions. The story in Acts 10 reads like a movie script as it goes back and forth between visions in two different places. It also reads like a blueprint of four principles for learning how to cross boundaries to share God's love.

PRINCIPLE #1
OTHER PEOPLE ARE LISTENING FOR GOD

Cornelius was in a noteworthy Gentile location—Caesarea. While not yet a convert to Jesus, Cornelius was a noteworthy Gentile—a "centurion," which means a leader of a hundred Roman soldiers. In spite of these two marks against him for those who were locked into boundaries, Cornelius was "a devout man who feared God" and who "gave alms generously" and who "prayed constantly to God" (Acts 10:2).

Jesus Creed love breaks down boundaries, but it can do so only when it recognizes that the God who loves us also loves everyone else. It is easy for us to be tempted to think that we alone are the right group, that we alone are the most faithful, and that others are less loved by God because we in fact love them less. But this gets things backward: we may love others less, but God loves them the same. Humans throughout the world and across the street listen for God because they, too, are *eikons* of God, humans made in God's image. Here is where we need to begin: with the recognition that everyone can be a seeker for God just as we are.

PRINCIPLE #2
RESISTANCE TO BOUNDARY-BREAKING
IS NORMAL

It's one thing to believe and think everyone can be a seeker for God. It's another thing to put this belief into practice. Even after Peter saw Jesus cross boundaries of all sorts, he had trouble crossing his own boundaries.

Peter, a good Jewish man who practiced kosher food laws, was hungry. He fell asleep, and in that sleep he saw a vision: God lowered down a picnic of food on a sheet in front of Peter's hungry body. But the oddest thing was that the sheet was filled with unclean animals. A voice (from God) told Peter to kill these animals and eat them. Peter responded by quoting the Bible back on God. But God told Peter that God was making some changes: "What God has made clean, you must not call profane" (Acts 10:15).

Perhaps you are like Peter. Perhaps you need to hear from God that the boundaries of your traditional faith need to be crossed because God is at work outside your boundaries. To practice the Jesus Creed means to muster the courage to break through boundaries.

PRINCIPLE #3
GOD IS IMPARTIAL

God had also been speaking to Cornelius about coming into the new family of God, so Cornelius sent some servants to invite Peter to his (Gentile) home. Peter, after experiencing his vision, realized that this invitation from a Gentile was something he needed to accept. When Peter arrived, met everyone, and heard the encounter of Cornelius with the God of Israel, Peter said: "God has shown me that I should not call anyone profane or unclean" (Acts 10:28). Then Peter uttered words that might reshape our lives today: "I truly understand that God shows no partiality, but in every nation anyone who fears him and does what is right is acceptable to him" (10:34–35).

The God worthy of the description that "God is love" (1 John 4:16) is the God who is not partial. Instead of thinking we are privileged, Peter urges us to welcome others into the privilege that breaks down the boundary of privilege.

PRINCIPLE #4
GOD DWELLS WITH ALL WHO FACE GOD

Once Peter explained the gospel to Cornelius, "the Holy Spirit fell upon all who heard the word" (Acts 10:44). Holy Spirit down-comings and outpourings and filling-ups happen when boundaries are crossed and when we knock down the walls of privilege to form the flat plain of community. God loves you; God loves me; God loves everyone. We extend the grace of the Jesus Creed when we listen to the good news that God is not a boundary-maker but a boundary-breaker.

———————

Facing this day:
The Jesus Creed calls us to knock down the boundary of privilege in order to extend the grace of God to others.

Scriptural focus:
"I truly understand that God shows no partiality, but in every nation anyone who fears him and does what is right is acceptable to him."
—Acts 10:34–35

PART 6

The Jesus Creed Becomes the Love Chapter

The Jesus Creed unleashed an early Christianity that sought to live a life of love daily. The most significant impact of the Jesus Creed on the apostle Paul was his elaboration of love in what we now call the Love Chapter, 1 Corinthians 13. Here we find the second half of the Jesus Creed expounded for a young congregation.

Gift-distributing Love

"If I speak in the tongues of mortals and of angels,
but do not have love,
I am a noisy gong or a clanging cymbal."
—1 Corinthians 13:1

The Love Chapter, 1 Corinthians 13, is one of the most beloved chapters in the whole Bible. Perhaps we need to remind ourselves that Paul wedged the Love Chapter between two chapters about spiritual gifts and relationships among Christians. The "gifts" Paul wrote about are the special talents Christians exercise that help the "body" (the local church). Paul mentioned these gifts by name: wisdom, knowledge, faith, healing, miracles, prophecy, discernment of spirits, speaking in tongues, and interpreting tongues (1 Corinthians 12:7–10). Paul instructed the Corinthians about these gifts, but right in the middle he stopped, grabbed their attention, and gave a little sermon on love. Love, he told them, drives the gifts or they cease being gifts.

We may be justifiably proud of the gifts God has given to us. We may delight in what God enables us to do. And we may be intoxicated with our fidelity to orthodoxy and our commitment to being right. We may "have" all these things and still, to quote Gordon Fee, our life "before God adds up to zero" if our gifts are not swept into love for others. If our spiritual gifts are not animated by love, they are little more than business transactions.

How can our gifts be shaped by loving others?

HOLD YOUR HANDS OUT BEFORE GOD TO RECEIVE YOUR GIFT AS A GIFT

Maybe we need to remind ourselves today that the gifts we have really are gifts—not something we created. Paul's words in chapter twelve makes this abundantly clear: "and there are varieties of activities, but it is the same God who activates all of them in everyone" (12:6). When you give a gift to someone, what does the receiver do? He or she simply reaches out and accepts the gift from you.

Billy Graham had the gift of evangelism, but he didn't become an evangelist by his own choice; Mother Teresa didn't get passion for the poor of Calcutta by application to the home office; and John Stott didn't grow up

knowing his name would become synonymous with clear
Bible teaching. To each of these God gave the gift of
evangelism, compassion, or preaching.

We might not be Billy Graham or Mother Teresa or
John Stott, but God has given each of us gifts. Let us
stretch out our arms with thanks to God, for God gave
these gifts to us. They are not ours; they are God's gifts to
us. We give thanks to God and his gracious love for what
we have received.

DISTRIBUTE OUR GIFT TO OTHERS

"To each is given the manifestation of the Spirit for the
common good," wrote Paul (1 Corinthians 12:7). Notice
those last four words, "for the common good." Spiritual
gifts are much like the money handled by tellers at a
bank: those coins and bills are not theirs to keep. They
are given the task to distribute the money to others.

Do our gifts bring attention to ourselves? Do our gifts
lead us to think we are special and important and even
perhaps indispensable? Are our gifts building a little name
for ourselves that we have given a "brand" and now are
"marketing"?

Paul wants us to see that we are distributors of grace.
God has given us something, not so we can bundle it all up
into safe storage for ourselves or market it to the world,

but so that we can give it as a gift to others. When we see ourselves as gift-distributors rather than gift-gatherers, we begin to exercise those gifts with a Jesus Creed kind of love.

BE MORE AWARE THAT EVERYONE ELSE HAS A GIFT, TOO

Perhaps we need to look around to see that we are not the only one with a gift from God. "To each is given the manifestation of the Spirit for the common good," Paul wrote (1 Corinthians 12:7). *To each.*

In football, some are asked to block, others to run, another to pass, and yet another to catch. Linemen don't grouse if they don't get to pass, and quarterbacks don't complain if they don't get to block. Each person has an assignment. When each person does their assignment, the team accomplishes its goals. The church is like a football team.

You and I are not the only ones who have an assignment-gift. Each of us has a spiritual assignment. Only when we see that our gift is part of the team called the body of Christ do we convert our gifts into the service of love for others.

Facing this day:
God empowers us to use our gifts in love for others.

Scriptural focus:
"All these [gifts] are activated by one and the same Spirit, who allots to each one individually just as the Spirit chooses."
—1 Corinthians 12:11

Love Is . . .

*"Love is patient; love is kind;
love is not envious or boastful or arrogant or
rude."*
—1 Corinthians 13:4–5

Love is . . . is the beginning to a sentence that many have filled in. What strikes me most about love in Paul's Love Chapter is that Jesus Creed love is *one hundred percent relational*. Paul says love is patient and it is kind and it is not envious or boastful or arrogant or rude. These are nice ideas and important words, but they do us no good if we don't realize that love comes into play only with other people.

Talking about the Love Chapter is sometimes like attending a missions rally where a missionary speaker comes in and generates enthusiasm about going to a remote location in the middle of a thick jungle filled with snakes. But when it comes to signing on the line to join the missionary society, or finding the funds to finance a missionary trip, or getting in the airplane to actually depart for that jungle, there's a real question about whether that enthusiasm will translate into reality.

Real love, the love for your neighbor that the Jesus Creed teaches, is what happens between two or more people in concrete reality. This is why what Paul says is so important: "Love is patient [with others]; love is kind [to others]; love is not envious [of others] or boastful [in front of others] or arrogant [in the face of others] or rude [to others]." These are virtues needed in the ordinary details of ordinary life.

LOVE IS PATIENT WITH OTHER PEOPLE

Patience is not hard to define, but patience is hard to put into practice. Here is a piece of advice from Paul in another letter: "And we urge you, beloved, to admonish the idlers, encourage the faint hearted, help the weak, be patient with all of them" (1 Thessalonians 5:14). Patience, the capacity to hold down one's anger under stress, endures lovingly the idler, the faint of heart, and the weak. Perhaps we need to be reminded that patience is not needed when everything is going swimmingly well. To be patient means we need to face God and ask God for the something extra.

Knowing how difficult it is to practice this call to patience, Paul points out that patience is a fruit of the Spirit's presence in us: "By contrast," he says in Galatians 5:22, "the fruit of the Spirit is . . . patience." The divine origins of the patience we are called to leads Paul to say our patience is actually God's strength at work in us: "May you be made strong with all the strength that comes from his glorious power, and may you be prepared to endure everything with patience" (Colossians 1:11).

As parents wait patiently for a child to put on a coat so the child can learn to accomplish tasks independently, as a teacher waits patiently as a student attempts to work through an idea, and as friends wait patiently for friends to discover the same interests, so we are called to wait with patience for those in our community who need time to become more mature.

LOVE IS KIND TO OTHER PEOPLE

Kindness differs from goodness in that the former emphasizes a goodness directed at someone who is undeserving and perhaps even unreceptive to the offer of goodness. A statement by Jesus makes clear what kindness means: "But love your enemies, do good, and lend, expecting nothing in return. Your reward will be great, and you will be children of the Most High; for he is *kind* to the ungrateful and the wicked" (Luke 6:35).

Christian kindness emerges, along with the Jesus Creed, from God's goodness to those who are unreceptive. Paul is not tooting his own horn when he describes his own kindness under trial; instead, he is magnifying the power of God's kindness at work in his own life. Ponder what he writes to the Corinthians in chapter six of his second letter, because here we see a sterling example of the patient love the Jesus Creed asks of us:

> [B]ut as servants of God we have commended ourselves in every way: through great endurance, in afflictions, hardships, calamities, beatings, imprisonments, riots, labors, sleepless nights, hunger; by purity, knowledge, *patience, kindness*, holiness of spirit, genuine love, truthful speech, and the power of God; with the weapons of righteousness for the right hand and for the left; in honor and dishonor, in ill repute and good repute. We are treated as impostors, and yet are true; as unknown, and yet are well known; as dying, and see—we are alive; as punished, and yet not killed; as sorrowful, yet always rejoicing; as poor, yet making many rich; as having nothing, and yet possessing everything.

We should perhaps learn to disconnect our genteel sense of niceness from what Paul means when he speaks of kindness. For Paul, to be kind is to respond to difficult situations in the power of God in such a way that the grace of God is put on display.

LOVE IS NOT ENVIOUS, BOASTFUL, ARROGANT, OR RUDE

Envy, which is the desire to have what others have, makes us either critical or competitive. If we are critical, we tear the other person down, and if we are competitive, we try to get ahead of the other person. In either case we are not happy with our lot in life or we are ticked with God for assigning our lot. We are also not happy with what God has done for the person of whom we are envious. But, if we see with love's eyes, we rejoice in where we are and where she is or he is.

Boasting establishes our superiority over someone else. We may inform someone of an accomplishment or an acquisition—say a new car—in order to inform them (which is fine) or to assert our superiority (which is boastful). Love buries our treasures and accomplishments until others dig them up.

Arrogance and rudeness are friends of envy and boasting. Both seek to establish our superiority, our being a cut above, at the expense of another. Instead of building bridges and establishing relationship as Jesus Creed love always does, these vices destroy relationships.

At Corinth there were wealthy Christians who made their supposed status clear at the Lord's Table—of all places! (1 Corinthians 11:22).

Love is what happens between people in concrete reality—when humans show patience and kindness, and avoid envy with one another—rather than simply the emotions that arise in one's mind or in one's heart. Madeleine L'Engle's *Wrinkle in Time* trilogy repeats the line, "Love isn't what you feel, it's what you do." Thinking about love or feeling loving are good; but the goal of love is to establish and maintain healthy relationships with others.

Facing this day:
Love is patient and kind in relationship with others; it is not envious of others.

Scriptural focus:
"Love is patient; love is kind; love is not envious or boastful or arrogant or rude."
—1 Corinthians 13:4–5

Love Denies the Self

Love "does not insist on its own way;
it is not irritable or resentful;
it does not rejoice in wrongdoing,
but rejoices in the truth."
—1 Corinthians 13:5–6

L ove orients us toward other people. We need to be oriented toward other people because we are naturally selfish. We want things our way, we get upset when things don't go our way, and we like to rub it in when someone doesn't want our way and gets their way and their way goes wrong. Which means we need to change. A life where relationships are shaped by the Jesus Creed involves change and transformation, because it makes room in our life for the lives of others.

It is in the heat of our own passions and wills that we are challenged to become loving people. As Roberta Bondi says so well, "The passions blind us so that we cannot love." She also observes that "only as we learn to love God and others do we gain the real freedom and autonomy in a society in which most people live in a state of slavery to their own needs and desires."

What the apostle Paul states in the Love Chapter is that the Jesus Creed's emphasis on loving others involves curbing our own passions, wills, and desires. Hence, he says, "[Love] does not insist on its own way; it is not irritable or resentful; it does not rejoice in wrongdoing, but rejoices in the truth" (1 Corinthians 13:5–6). Loving others, in other words, mirrors Jesus' call to self-denial (Luke 9:23).

LOVE DOESN'T INSIST ON ITS OWN WAY

Choosing between a life dedicated to the self and a life dedicated to loving the other is like coming upon a fork in a road. Jesus told those who were listening that to follow him led them on a path with a sign that read, "Follow Me, No More Self-Following." Paul expounds this very idea when he says that love "does not insist on its own way" (1 Corinthians 13:5).

Under the surface of every positive decision is a choice, a surge leading as well to a negative decision. To choose to live a life of loving others is to choose against a life of loving only ourselves. The paradigm for love's not insisting on its own way was potently expressed by Jesus in

Gethsemane when he prayed these words: "Abba, Father, for you all things are possible; remove this cup from me; yet, not what I want, but what you want" (Mark 14:36). As François Fénelon put it, "The true union with God is to do his will without ceasing in every duty of life, in spite of all natural disinclination, and however disagreeable or mortifying it may be to our self will." Love, because it is oriented toward the good of another, by nature says "no" to self-preoccupation.

LOVE IS NOT EASILY ANGERED

Anger is not a problem for all of us. For those who seem to fly off the handle (and we know who we are), for those who are easily irritated by the smallest of quirks, and for those who make others uncomfortable because of what simmers under the surface, the apostle Paul wrote one simple reminder: "love is not irritable." *Today's New International Version of the Bible* translates the expression this way: love "is not easily angered." Anger is not consistent with love because love creates an environment of safety, goodness, and compassion for the other person. A Jesus Creed kind of love is not angered because anger attempts to obliterate the other.

LOVE TAKES PLEASURE IN THE
FLOWERING OF TRUTH

The Message translates 1 Corinthians 13:5–6 with three potent lines:

> Love . . .　Doesn't keep score of the sins of others,
> Doesn't revel when others grovel,
> Takes pleasure in the flowering of truth.

Whether it is in our relationship with those we love the most, our relationship with our co-workers or with our neighbors or with our friends, central to the health of those relationships is the part our memory of wrongs plays. When you see someone, do you remember what they did to you long ago? Are you permitting your relationship to be defined by an injustice? Keeping score is not the way of love.

Neither is reveling when the other person experiences a wrong. One need not verbalize this for it to be true. The subtle delight, the inner satisfaction, or even the casual heartfelt smile when we see what has happened to another person is not the way of love.

Instead, the person who lives the Jesus Creed "rejoices in the truth." Love simply is happy and blesses God whenever something good happens to anyone—no matter who it might be that experiences that goodness.

Facing this day:
Love calms the self for the good of the other.

Scriptural focus:
"Then [Jesus] said to them all, 'If any want to become my followers, let them deny themselves and take up their cross daily and follow me.' "
—Luke 9:23

DAY 32

The Optimism of Love

"It bears all things,
believes all things,
hopes all things,
endures all things."
—1 Corinthians 13:7

True love—and you can't get around this one—is optimistic. The American novelist and essayist James Brach Cabell once said, "The optimist proclaims that we live in the best of all possible worlds; and the pessimist fears this is true." And Mark Twain once said that the "man who is a pessimist before 48 knows too much; if he is an optimist after it, he knows too little." Most of us know the delight of comparing and contrasting optimists and pessimists, but in that word "love" there is an unshakable, undeterred optimism. Love hopes for the intimate exchange with another person.

But the optimism of love is not a mental trick, as if by thinking positively only good things will happen. The optimism that comes from a Jesus Creed kind of love becomes optimistic because it believes and hopes in God. Perhaps you are facing a situation where the only realistic solution is either pessimistic or at least "realistic." Perhaps Paul's words, quoted above, need a fresh look. Love, Paul says, "believes all things" and "hopes all things."

OPTIMISTIC LOVE BELIEVES AND HOPES

The four lines quoted from 1 Corinthians at the head of today's reading are best understood from the middle out: believing and hoping give rise to bearing and enduring.

[Love] bears all things,
believes all things,
hopes all things,
endures all things.

What is it that the optimism of love believes? That good always happens? No, that would be contrary to everything we know and experience. That a cheery outlook on life makes the sky bluer? Perhaps it does, but that is surely not Paul's point. Or that if we believe hard enough, what we want most will happen? This would make us in charge of the world. No, what Paul has in mind is far more profound.

The optimistic love Paul teaches is an optimism that emerges from believing and hoping in God. Three thoughts shape Paul's optimism: God's unending, unstoppable, unconditional love; the fact that Good Friday gave way to Easter morn; and the reality that God's Spirit was now unleashed in humans to empower them to become the "new creation." Because of the Father's love, the Son's victory, and the Spirit's power, genuine love can believe and hope that somehow, someday, things will change.

OPTIMISTIC LOVE BEARS AND ENDURES

Abraham believed and hoped in God, so he endured the long trek from the Fertile Crescent to the Land that became Israel. Moses believed and hoped in the God who liberated Israel from Egypt, so he endured forty years in the wilderness as God prepared Israel for the Land. David believed and hoped in the God who called him to be king, so he endured years of exile and hiding. The prophets believed and hoped in the God who ended exiles, so they endured waiting before they returned to the Land. Jesus believed and hoped in his Father, so he endured the cross. The apostle Paul believed and hoped in the God of the gospel, so he endured suffering to extend the gospel's power throughout the Roman Empire.

Love that flows from God is love that believes and

hopes and bears and endures. What strikes me about the biblical examples above is how long those who believed endured before they got what they hoped for. Mother Teresa, so we are now learning, endured decades of the dark night of the soul because she believed and hoped in God, even when she thought that God was not listening.

The optimistic love of Paul endures. Why? Because a Jesus Creed kind of love so loves the other person that it can't let go. When Don Marquis, an American humorist, said that "an optimist is a guy that has never had much experience," he was speaking from a lack of experience with the kind of love Paul knew.

Facing this day:
Love is hopeful because of God.

Scriptural focus:
"And not only that, but we also boast in our sufferings, knowing that suffering produces endurance, and endurance produces character, and character produces hope, and hope does not disappoint us, because God's love has been poured into our hearts through the Holy Spirit that has been given to us."
—Romans 5:3–5

DAY 33

A Love Kind of Life

"Love never ends."
—1 Corinthians 13:8

The two most profound questions I have ever been asked by a student are these: First, what was God doing before creation? Second, what will we do in heaven? Here is my answer of faith: At the Beginning of all beginnings the God of the perichoresis enjoyed the delight of love within the community called Trinity, and at the End of all ends will be the ongoing love of the Trinity as we participate in that love.

Think about the first one first. If before creation all that existed was God in Three Persons—Father, Son, and Holy Spirit—what were the Three-in-One doing? They were madly in love with One Another in the endless mutual enjoyment of One Another. Before Creation was the divine dance of joyful, holy love.

And, if in eternity past the Three Persons were endlessly enjoying One Another in the dance of love, in eternity future they will do the same—for that enjoyment of love is what God is according to the Bible. This means that we will be caught up in the endless dance of the Trinity's love for all eternity. Think about it: if love is what happened before creation and if love is what happens in eternity, then love never ends.

If love—for God, for self, and for others—never ends, then we need to map out a life for ourselves that prepares us for the perichoretic dance of the Trinity. All too often we hear in Christian circles that what is eternal is heaven, or we hear a preacher promising us "eternal life" or heaven. Both of these are true, but not quite true enough. What is finally eternal is love, and *heaven* and *eternal life* are terms that house what is truly eternal: love.

LOVE INSPIRES HOPE

If the end is love, we can have hope for that Love-End. The apostle Paul furnishes us with a great example of this in 1 Corinthians 15:24. Notice these words: "Then comes the *end*," Paul says. And what will happen? Jesus Christ then "hands over the kingdom to God the Father, after he has destroyed every ruler and every authority and power." Paul speaks here of systemic injustices, of rulers who abuse their powers and their authority by inflicting violence. The person who loves in hope also longs for the ending of violence and injustice.

But there is one enemy that Paul has his special sights on: "The last enemy to be destroyed is death" (15:26). Rulers might break up love, but can death put an end to love? Is death the last word? The good news of the gospel is that the Omega Point is not death. The final word beyond all words is Love.

Because the final word is Love, we can face today with love. We can commit ourselves to a life of love—for God, for ourselves, and for others—because the end is love.

LOVE INSPIRES GIVING

When the end comes, when love utters that final word, we see something that sets a pattern for all of life. In the verses quoted above we read this: "Then comes the end, when [Jesus Christ] hands over the kingdom to God the Father." The last word that ushers us into eternity is an action: the Son, whose mission it was to bring the kingdom of God, *gives the kingdom to the Father.* The last word is the action of giving.

Here we find the secret to our joy in giving. Who doesn't enjoy giving? Whether it is a birthday card or a bundle of flowers or money to someone in need or a book for a special friend or a kind letter of encouragement to someone we barely know, we like giving; but why do we enjoy it so much? Because the essence of giving is love. The secret to the joy of giving is that giving partakes in eternity, it expresses in concrete form the final utterance of life, and it shares in the Son's giving to the Father.

Whatever you are privileged today to give in the name of love participates in that final action of love, the giving of all we have back to the God who is Love.

Facing this day:
Every act of love today participates in eternal love.

Scriptural focus:
"Therefore, my beloved, be steadfast, immovable, always excelling in the work of the Lord, because you know that in the Lord your labor is not in vain."
—1 Corinthians 15:58

DAY 34

The End of Gifts

*"But as for prophecies, they will
come to an end;
as for tongues, they will cease;
as for knowledge, it will come to an end."*
—1 Corinthians 13:8

At some point, the most cherished gifts you bring to the table will be swallowed into love.

Most of us connect what we do with who we are. Most of us associate our worth with our gifts. Our gifts are a gift from God, and God gives us these gifts—whatever it is that God has assigned us to do—for the good of others. But what we *do* is not eternal. What is eternal is the relationship these gifts establish.

Here are Paul's words about spiritual gifts in the middle of his discussion about spiritual gifts: "But as for prophecies, they will come to an end; as for tongues, they will cease; as for knowledge, it will come to an end." Our gifts are what we do. But what we do will "come to an end" the way an architect's plans and blueprints create a cathedral, the way a parent's efforts create a healthy adult, and the way a small group leader's study and questions create patterns for worship and spiritual formation. When the cathedral is dedicated, when the child establishes an independent life, and when the small group participant grows in grace, the "gift" has reached its goal.

All that we do, Paul says, will end. Where will it end? In love.

OUR GIFTS FORGE RELATIONSHIPS

Traveling on an airplane after a conference with other professors, I found myself sitting next to a professor, Dr. Julius Scott, who was in his last year of teaching. He was a fine teacher, and I know this because he taught my daughter at Wheaton. We chatted about his specialty of teaching New Testament and how he was able to bring his love for archaeology into the classroom to excite students about the world of Jesus and the early Christians. He reminisced about his decades of teaching. He then began to talk about what he liked most and what he would miss. So I asked him the obvious: "What will you miss most?" He said two words: "My students." Then he began to weep quietly.

For ten minutes we sat in utter silence, about 30,000 feet above the Pennsylvania hills, as Dr. Scott experienced what every teacher I know someday will experience: the utter joy of our relationships with students. Julius loved the technicalities of archaeology and organizing notes for lectures and answering student questions and inspiring students to root their faith in the realities of the Bible. But what he most loved was the students. He liked teaching; but he loves his students.

OUR RELATIONSHIPS WILL REMAIN

"Love never ends." Prophecy—the gift of speaking for God, tongue-speaking—the gift of heavenly communication, and knowledge—the gift of making known what the body needs to know, each has a goal, and when that goal is reached, the gift gives way to love.

Gifts, Paul tells us in 1 Corinthians 13:12, will end when we are known as we are meant to be known by God and by others: "For now we see in a mirror, dimly, but then we will see face to face. Now I know only in part; then I will know fully, even as I have been fully known." The relationship with God and with others that gifts forge is what will remain.

EXERCISE YOUR GIFTS TO ESTABLISH
THOSE RELATIONSHIPS

It is easy for us to think that who we are is what we do. What we do, to be sure, is a gift from God. But Paul reminds us that what we do has a goal: to establish and nurture what will remain. What will remain is love. Let us begin today to see our gifts, not just as the enjoyment of our contribution to the good of the church but also as that which will lead us all into what will never end: love.

———————

Facing this day:
Our spiritual gifts are given to nurture what will remain forever: love.

Scriptural focus:
"Now I know only in part; then I will know fully, even as I have been fully known."
—1 Corinthians 13:12

The Greatest of These Is Love

"And now faith, hope, and love abide,
these three; and the greatest of these is love."
—1 Corinthians 13:13

J esus taught his followers that there was no commandment greater than the two commandments to love God and to love others. Paul, without quoting the Jesus Creed once in the Love Chapter, explored the meaning of the Jesus Creed for church life and seemed to hint at the very words of Jesus when he wrote that "the greatest of these is love." Indeed, the greatest of our responsibilities is to love, and since for Paul love was about relationships, we can fill in the blanks and say that the "greatest of these is to love God and others."

But for "now," Paul's words remind us, we live by faith and with hope and in love. Because "now" the End has not yet come, because now the final consummation of pure Love has not yet reached us, we live by faith and with hope and in love because we anticipate that day. A life dedicated to the Jesus Creed kind of love is an ongoing act of faith and hope.

BY FAITH

Faith is the act of trusting God to be good to his word. God's word is that redemption is found in the life, death, and resurrection of Jesus Christ, and God's word is also that we can find new creation through the Holy Spirit. Paul summons us to trust that good word of God. You can't set up an experiment in a laboratory of humans who are messed up, squirt a few drops of faith in their test tube, and prove the truth of the gospel. Instead, faith means trusting God at his word and letting the good word of God transform how we live. As Paul says in 2 Corinthians 5:7, "for we walk by faith, not by sight." The Christian knows that God is love and that in the end love will prevail; and the Christian devotes herself or himself to a life of love because of faith in God's truthful word.

WITH HOPE

I love Paul's thumbnail sketch of hope in Romans 8:24: "For in hope we were saved. Now hope that is seen is not hope. For who hopes for what is seen?" Once again, we can't prove that injustices will eventually be undone, or that violence will be wiped off the map, or that racism will give way to love—even if we have a great example in South Africa. But, like Abraham—"Hoping against hope, he believed that he would become 'the father of many nations' " (Romans 4:18)—we are called to press forward in light of God's promise and in the teeth sometimes of the odds coming against us. We hope for justice in this world, and we live as if that kingdom of justice were already here, because Jesus taught us to pray, "Your kingdom come. Your will be done, on earth as it is in heaven" (Matthew 6:10). A Jesus Creed kind of love acts on this in hope.

IN LOVE

To understand what Paul means by love let me now try on a definition. Love of others means to yearn for, pray for, and work for the other person so that they can become the person God wants them to be and do what God wants them to do. The nitty-gritty reality of love for Paul, rooting his entire chapter as he does in the Jesus Creed, is a love that cares so much about others that it refuses to limit itself to merely tolerating the other person. It moves beyond the nicety of toleration to engage the other person to follow Jesus by entering the kingdom where the Jesus Creed is both established and transforms all of life.

BUT . . . IN THE END

In 1 Corinthians 13's closing verse, Paul says we "now" live by faith, with hope, and in love. But, in the "end," only love will remain. It is the greatest of these three. Why? Because before there was an "In the beginning," there was a divine community of love that delighted in the constant call to One Another of these words: "Come, my Beloved." Ultimately, there was and will be one thing: endless delight in God's love and the overflow of joy as we enter into that love forever.

———————

Facing this day:
We live the love of the Jesus Creed by faith and with hope.

Scriptural focus:
"And now faith, hope, and love abide, these three; and the greatest of these is love."
—1 Corinthians 13:13

PART 7

Examples of Jesus Creed Love

There are many wonderful examples of living the Jesus Creed in the pages of the New Testament. We will look at five of these and see that love takes on various shapes.

Love Is Supporting

"The twelve were with [Jesus],
as well as some women who had been cured of
evil spirits and infirmities:
Mary, called Magdalene, from whom seven
demons had gone out,
and Joanna, the wife of Herod's steward Chuza,
and Susanna, and many others,
who provided for them out of their resources."
—Luke 8:1–3

Jesus had an entourage. Luke tells us that "twelve were with him, as well as some women who had been cured of evil spirits and infirmities: Mary, called Magdalene, from whom seven demons had gone out, and Joanna, the wife of Herod's steward Chuza, and Susanna, and many others, who provided for them out of their resources" (Luke 8:1–3). It's one thing to enter a Galilean village alone or with a few followers, it's quite another to enter with what appears (in these verses) to be twenty or thirty disciples, over half of whom appear to be women!

We don't know what these women did, but we do know one important thing: some were wealthy enough to provide for Jesus and his followers "out of their resources." Jesus expected his followers to support the work of God. Love supports the work of God. Supporting Jesus turns one's love for Jesus and for his kingdom vision and for his followers into living reality. When Jesus called his followers to love God and to love others, involved in that love was the willingness to use resources for kingdom work.

MONEY MATTERS TO JESUS

Many in our world are irritated by radio preachers and televangelists asking for money, if not by their own local pastor when he does the same thing. Many are justifiably bothered by where "church funds" go—to build bigger buildings that might not always be needed, to finance activities that may not always be wise, or to support a program that can suggest extravagance. Criticisms notwithstanding, there remains a point: what we do with our money reveals what matters to us.

Jesus was concerned and candid about a person's wealth and money. "No slave can serve two masters," Jesus said. Why? "For a slave will either hate the one and love the other, or be devoted to the one and despise the other. You cannot serve God and wealth [money]"

(Luke 16:13). Jesus' candor was shown clearly when he challenged Zacchaeus (Luke 19:1–10) and the rich young ruler (18:18–30) to give up their goods for the benefit of others. And one of the most electric examples of the power of the Spirit in using funds to love others in the early church was shown when, after Pentecost, the Jerusalem community pooled their resources to support the work of God (Acts 2:42–47).

Money matters because it reveals both what we want to hold onto and what we value enough to support.

YOUR MONEY ALSO MATTERS TO JESUS

Because money matters, and because your money matters, you need to be wise about where it goes. Some of it, of course, goes for your needs. But wise people don't spend to the extreme end of their income (or beyond it), but instead both spend and save. In addition, they also give out of love for others. In fact, wise people advise others that giving comes first, saving second, and spending third.

Many of us are touchy about this subject of supporting the work of God with our financial resources, so let's think about this with level heads and generous hearts. The work of God begins in our local community of faith and spreads across the globe, and most of us know of God-work that we can support—such as special ministries at our church; local social outreach groups; Christian ministries throughout the world; global ministries that care for people who have AIDS or who are impoverished, or that provide education where it needs to be boosted, or that provide for basic health care and proper water supplies where there is a need.

The women around Jesus valued him and his followers and what he was doing enough to pick up their bags with their funds so they could travel with and support Jesus.

This is the kind of pulse you may have heard repeatedly from Jesus: "Sell your possessions, and give alms. Make purses for yourselves that do not wear out, an unfailing treasure in heaven, where no thief comes near and no moth destroys. For where your treasure is, there your heart will be also" (Luke 12:33–34). These women heard Jesus say things like this and they acted on it.

Facing this day:
Love supports the work of God.

Scriptural focus:
"But strive first for the kingdom of God and his righteousness, and all these things will be given to you as well."
—Matthew 6:33

DAY 37

Love Serves

*"Through Silvanus, whom I consider
a faithful brother,
I have written this short letter
to encourage you and to testify
that this is the true grace of God."*
—1 Peter 5:12

High honors are deserved by those who labor behind the scenes, whose assignment is to perform tasks behind the counter, who see that the routine chore is accomplished, and whose names are rarely known, but without whom the task would not get done. The most exalted form of love is service.

At our school there is an abundance of such folks, but I'd like to mention one. Susie Olsen attended North Park a few decades back and has since labored behind the scenes with Christian grace, cheerfulness, kindness, and diligence. She is now the administrative assistant to our Dean, but her name is rarely mentioned when one of our major objectives is reached. Without her, many tasks would not get off the ground or be completed. She, and others like her, makes our school tick. Rarely, though, do such people get the credit they deserve.

Serving, whether behind the scenes or not, is the most exalted form of love the Bible knows of. Love in the Bible consists in giving oneself to the other, and the giving of oneself defines the term "service." What the early Christians realized was that service was not just for those behind the scenes—it was the designed mode of life for every Christian, including the leaders.

AN EARLY CHRISTIAN POSTMAN

An early Christian who gave himself for others was Silvanus, who learned to serve his fellow followers of Christ even as a leader. He was prominent enough to be one of the writers of both letters to the Thessalonians, for he shows up in the first verse of each of the letters to the churches in Thessalonica. Paul says Silvanus was a preacher of the gospel (2 Corinthians 1:19), and the book of Acts mentions him as a prominent leader (Acts 15:22, 27, 32, where he is called by the Greek form of his name, "Silas").

But Silvanus's prominence did not excuse him from serving an apostle. Peter wrote his letter "through

Silvanus." This means either Silvanus converted Peter's speech into written letters—acting as his secretary or amanuensis—or (which is more likely) he was Peter's courier or postman. Even though he was a prominent leader of the church, Silvanus served Peter for the good of the gospel, carrying Peter's letter from Rome to Asia Minor. In fact, Silvanus may have acquired the reputation as a professional, Christian postman, for he also carried the letter written by the entire Jerusalem church to the church at Antioch (Acts 15:22, 30). Surely it was a mark of honor both to carry and then also to interpret the apostle's letter when read, but this should not detract from the service of spending weeks on the road and sea, often including the nuisance of waiting for available ships, for the spread of the gospel.

SERVING OTHERS IS WHAT LOVE IS ALL ABOUT

"Servant" is one of the greatest of Christian words used as a label for a variety of Christians. The fountainhead for who gets called "servant" begins with Jesus, who said he did not come to be served but to serve (Mark 10:45). Then the earliest ministerial office in the church was for "deacons," a Greek word (*diakonos*) for those appointed to serve others (Acts 6:1–6). Within a decade or two after the resurrection of Jesus, the most elevated label among early Christians was to be called a "servant." We see this in Paul when he says he is "a servant of Jesus Christ" (Romans 1:1).

The choice of "servant" as a label of elevation tells the Christian story itself. The story is that the Father and Son and Spirit are constantly giving themselves in service to One Another, and the Father gave his Son to be the Servant, and that life—a life of loving service for others—creates an entirely new way of looking at the Jesus Creed kind of love we find in the New Testament. Love is an act of serving the other: husbands serving wives and wives serving husbands, and neighbors serving one another, and pastors calling themselves "ministers" (which is a dignified translation of "servant").

Perhaps we need to join Jesus to realize that serving another is the most elevated form of life we can find, and that service is the essence of our love for others. Recently Kris and I met with a local pastor, the Reverend Patti Snickenberger. A few times during our conversation, she asked us, "What can I do to help you?" Far more serving than the normal comment, "If you need us, give us a call," Patti's question is for us the model question of the Christian.

However, if we do ask Patti's question, we will need to be ready for someone to give us an answer that will provide us with an opportunity to serve. Then we will be given the opportunity to follow the path of the earliest Christians—who knew that love meant service.

———————

Facing this day:
Serving others is the Christian form of love.

Scriptural focus:
"But Jesus called them to him and said, 'You know that the rulers of the Gentiles lord it over them, and their great ones are tyrants over them. It will not be so among you; but whoever wishes to be great among you must be your servant, and whoever wishes to be first among you must be your slave.' "
—Matthew 20:25–27

Affirming Love

"For [Phoebe] has been a benefactor
of many and of myself as well."
—Romans 16:2

L ove affirms others because love publicly declares its support for someone else. Affirmation creates a wave of considered appreciation of others. We are wise to avoid flattery and insincere affirmations, but otherwise, the Jesus Creed shapes the kind of love that leads to the open acknowledgment of others. Generous acknowledgment of another's giftedness visibly maps out the virtue of others and charts an example for others to follow.

Dignity and gratitude are at the heart of a Jesus Creed kind of affirmation. In loving a fellow Christian we openly recognize the person God made him or her to be, and we also acknowledge the contribution that person is making to the redemptive work of God in our world. Furthermore, affirmation requires the willingness to dethrone our own egos, for in acknowledging the dignity of the person and expressing gratitude for him or her, we affirm that their calling supplies what we need. The ultimate form of Christian affirmation can be found in the exercise of spiritual gifts in the Christian church: we each bring something to the table but, while at the table, we receive the benefit of the gifts of others.

Notice how Paul openly acknowledged Phoebe: "For [Phoebe] has been a benefactor of many and of myself as well" (Romans 16:2). Here the great apostle affirmed a female leader and her gifts. Phoebe was from the church in Cenchreae, the eastern port of Corinth in Greece, and Paul urged the Christians to offer Phoebe a place of shelter when she arrived in Rome. Phoebe, scholar Robert Jewett reminds us, should be given hospitality in Rome "with honors suitable to her position as a congregational leader, her previous contributions to the Christian mission, and her role in the missionary project envisioned in Rome." No one disputes Paul's status in the earliest churches, but what is sometimes overlooked is that he was also a spreader of "good gossip," because he affirmed others. There are all kinds of reasons to imitate Paul, so let's observe four attributes of Phoebe he affirmed.

AFFIRM GENDERS

It does not take a professional historian to know the public ministries of the church have been populated by males. Whether or not your community of faith continues that practice doesn't matter for the moment: both genders need to be affirmed. Phoebe was a woman of significance in the early church, probably the one who was the postwoman of the letter to the Romans, and Paul went out of his way to sing her praises. She was a "sister" of Paul because the church is a family, and each person in a family gets equal affirmation.

AFFIRM OFFICES

Phoebe was called a "deacon." Because the Pastoral letters seem to indicate that deacons were males whose wives seemed to serve along with their husbands, some prefer to translate the word "deacon" in Romans 16:1 as "deaconess," but this is unwise. The word Paul used for Phoebe in this verse is the Greek word *diakonos*, which means "deacon" (not "deaconess"). Furthermore, in the early churches this word implied that a person had an "office"—an officially designated ministry of serving, supporting, financing, leading, and pastoring—in the local church. Paul affirmed Phoebe for the office she held, for the service of leadership she provided, and acknowledged her diaconate.

AFFIRM VIRTUE

Phoebe was to be shown the hospitality deserving of the "saints." This indicates her moral virtue, her progress in sanctity, her commitment to following Jesus, and her moral stamina. Virtue needs to be affirmed in public. In our world perhaps the most distinctive form of affirming virtue is dedicating effort to writing a biography of a virtuous person, or holding up someone's autobiography as a story that charts the path of the Christian life. There are so many good examples of this, but I'll simply mention Lauren Winner's oft-read story *Girl Meets God*, Mother Teresa's intense journals and letters called *Come Be My Light,* and Virginia Stem Owens's *Caring for Mother: A Daughter's Long Goodbye*. Memoirs and biographies, especially when they tell the truth about a person, map virtue for others as they affirm the other person. Even more, virtues are best taught in storied form rather than by a simple list of rules to keep.

AFFIRM SPECIFIC MINISTRIES

Paul used a special term for Phoebe: she was a "benefactor," which means she was a woman of means who provided her home as the place for Christian fellowship in Cenchreae. This term also means she used her resources to further the work of God's kingdom.

Like the women who provided for Jesus and his apostles, Phoebe carried on the noble tradition of serving the kingdom of God by financial support.

Facing this day:
Love affirms others.

Scriptural focus:
"I commend to you our sister Phoebe, a deacon of the church at Cenchreae."
—Romans 16:1

Love Uses Its Voice
for Jesus

*"He must increase,
but I must decrease."*
—John 3:30

People at the time of Jesus at least wondered noble
things about John the Baptist. In one of the earliest
glimpses of the earliest days of Jesus, now found
in the second half of the first chapter of John's Gospel,
we read that some wondered if John the Baptist was the
"Messiah" or "Elijah" come back to life, or even a prophet
like Moses (1:19–21). To be asked if you are the Messiah
or Elijah or a prophet was noble indeed! When they finally
cornered John and asked him, "Who are you?" all he said
was this: "I am the *voice* of one crying in the wilderness"
(1:23). Imagine how tempting it might have been for John
to hear these great things said about him. It was like being
asked if you are the next Mother Teresa or Billy Graham
or the next Archbishop of Canterbury! John the Baptist

had no doubt heard his father, Zechariah, talk about what God was going to do through him [John] (Luke 1:67–79). But, when John was put on the line, John did not think about his own fame. Instead, he used his voice for Jesus.

The noblest thing that can be said of John is what he said of himself: he was a *voice* that spoke about Jesus. His love for God led him to speak of Jesus and point people to Jesus.

The words in John 3:30 are an example of what it means to live the Jesus Creed, of what it means to love God and to love others by using one's voice to point to the source of that love. When John was pressed a second time about what scriptural role he was to fulfill, he simply said, "He [Jesus] must increase, but I must decrease." John wasn't put on the stage for his few years of ministry to attract attention to himself, to make a name for himself, or to lead others into thinking he was great. He was here to speak about Jesus—he was the "voice."

So, let's point to Jesus by following John with our voices. To do this we will first need to read about Jesus until his words and life and death and resurrection saturate our bones. To learn to put into practice the Jesus Creed of loving others by pointing them to Jesus, we will need to begin by learning to love God. There is no better way to learn how to love God than to enter into the story of Jesus by reading the Gospels.

BY READING ABOUT JESUS

There are four Gospels, the first three called the "Synoptic" Gospels because there is so much similarity one can read them "synoptically" (together). And there is the Gospel of John. I suggest that you read them one by one first, starting with Matthew and finishing with John. As you read them, let their words wash over you and fill you with the words of Jesus.

Faith-shaped reading of the Gospels is not the same as "consumerist" reading. In the latter we gobble up a book, put it away, and find another to gobble away. In a faith-based reading, we read and listen and pause and pray and ponder and relish and chew and digest and wonder and pray some more. The Christian philosopher Paul J. Griffiths says this so well in his book *Religious Reading*: in religious reading we "read as a lover reads, with a tensile attentiveness that wishes to linger, to prolong, to savor, and has no interest at all in the quick orgasm of consumption." Religious reading wants not only to learn about Jesus but also to meditate on him so much that he enters into the soul and sinews of who we are and how we live. To use an image from another writer, Eugene Peterson, a faith-shaped reading reads in order to *Eat This Book*.

BY TALKING ABOUT JESUS

John lived a life of loving God by using his voice for Jesus. His way of pointing to Jesus provides indicators for us for using our own voices for Jesus to express our love both for God and for others. First, John pointed out the injustices of his society as inconsistent with the kingdom Jesus was bringing. Observe how similar John's call is to the call of Jesus in the Sermon on the Mount. Here are John's vibrant words from Luke 3:10–14:

> And the crowds asked him, "What then should we do?" In reply he said to them, "Whoever has two coats must share with anyone who has none; and whoever has food must do likewise." Even tax collectors came to be baptized, and they asked him, "Teacher, what should we do?" He said to them, "Collect no more than the amount prescribed for you." Soldiers also asked him, "And we, what should we do?" He said to them, "Do not extort money from anyone by threats or false accusation, and be satisfied with your wages."

Surely we can do no less than John by calling attention to the injustices of our world that are at odds with the kingdom ethic of the Jesus Creed.

Not only did John use his voice to point out injustices, but also he spoke of the powerful life that can come by turning to Jesus. "I baptize you," John declared, "with water; but one who is more powerful than I is coming. . . . He will baptize you with the Holy Spirit and fire" (Luke 3:16). This Spirit-and-fire baptism Jesus would bring was in part filled by Pentecost—where God's people were empowered by the Spirit to witness mightily to Jesus Christ and to put into practice the ethic of the Jesus Creed.

John's voice points the way for our voices: we can use our voices to point others to justice and to God's power to live the Jesus Creed.

Facing this day:
To love God and others is to use our voices
to point to Jesus.

Scriptural focus:
"Now among those who went up to worship at the festival were some Greeks. They came to Philip, who was from Bethsaida in Galilee, and said to him, 'Sir, we wish to see Jesus.'"
—John 12:20–21

Jesus Creed Grace

*"When they had finished breakfast, Jesus said
to Simon Peter,
'Simon son of John, do you love me more than
these?'
He said to him, 'Yes, Lord; you know that I
love you.'
Jesus said to him, 'Feed my lambs.' "*
—John 21:15

The Jesus Creed is an ideal—an ideal of loving God with everything we've got and loving others in a life of service. The reality is that we don't always live the Jesus Creed. It is important, then, to finish *40 Days Living the Jesus Creed* on a note of grace. What happens when we fail to follow the Jesus Creed? One of the grander flashes of grace in the pages of the Bible is that those who are most often heroized are also painted with realism. It is this realism that reminds us of the gospel that gives rise to the Jesus Creed. Each of us who seeks to live the Jesus Creed fails. The gospel reminds us that our failures are not the final word. The final word is grace that forgives and restores. This grace of forgiveness can be found in the examples of some characters in the Gospels.

MISTAKES WE MAKE

Mary, John, and Peter each took missteps as they learned to walk on the path of the Jesus Creed. Mary, who had more than her share of private revelations of who her Son would be, discovered at a wedding that the wine supply was running short. So she stepped up to Jesus to demand that he do something about it. Jesus rebuffed her aggression for the moment; she stepped back in realization that Jesus would do things when his Father said so, and she learned from her mistake (John 2:1–10). John, who later called himself the "beloved disciple"—the one Jesus loved specially—took a few missteps himself, including one time hoping God would incinerate a Samaritan village for not responding to the gospel on first hearing (Luke 9:51–56). Peter, Jesus' lead apostle, denied Jesus flat-out when the heat was on (Mark 14:66–72). Failure accompanies anyone who seeks to live by the Jesus Creed, but the gospel word of Jesus is the word of grace.

AFTER MAKING MISTAKES

The pages of the Gospels reveal a pattern of grace. In general, those who live the Jesus Creed follow Jesus. But, whether it is because they don't understand or are fearful or choose the wrong thing, followers of Jesus make mistakes. The Bible uses words like "sin" and "transgress" for missteps in loving God, self, and others. The good news of the Gospels is that Jesus dealt with his followers who failed with two clear directives: first, he told them they did wrong. When John and his brother wanted to be the MVPs of the kingdom community, Jesus rebuked them for their wrong ambitions and passions (Mark 10:35–40). Jesus always followed the first directive with the second directive, the word of grace and forgiveness: after his disciples failed, he urged them to resume following him again (10:41–45).

The pattern is very simple: for those who fail, there is the word of rebuke followed by the word of grace to get back on the path. That word of grace involves forgiveness and restoration. Isn't this why John, who knew failure firsthand, reminded his readers that God is forgiving and that they needed but to confess their sins (1 John 1:9), and why he exhorted his readers so often to continue in love?

This pattern of Jesus Creed grace reminds us that behind the Jesus Creed is not a law-giving, stern God but a grace-giving, gospel God who not only gave himself to his Son in never-ending love, but also gave that same Son to us so that we might be drawn into the never-ending love of God.

Facing this day:
Behind the Jesus Creed is Jesus Creed grace.

Scriptural focus:
"Jesus answered, 'The first is, "Hear, O Israel: the Lord our God, the Lord is one; you shall love the Lord your God with all your heart, and with all your soul, and with all your mind, and with all your strength." The second is this, "You shall love your neighbor as yourself." There is no other commandment greater than these.'"
—Mark 12:29–31

After Words

Lil Copan, my editor and friend, called me some months back and asked if I would be willing to extend *The Jesus Creed: Loving God, Loving Others* into a different book with a new format. I am grateful to her and the good folks at Paraclete Press for this creative invitation. The Jesus Creed was not just something Jesus taught; it was something the apostles also taught. So this book gave me the opportunity to extend the scope of the original book into the first generation of Christians, those who followed Jesus and carried his message across the ancient world.

Before Lil puts her green pen to my prose, first Kris reads it and makes her many suggestions. Kris has managed somehow to deepen our love while also pointing out the weakness of a paragraph or an idea here and there. That combination of kindness and firmness was made clear one summer evening when she said, "I don't know how to say this, Scot, but this chapter isn't even interesting." The next day I rewrote the whole chapter. I won't tell you which chapter it was.

Kris also made the suggestion that we dedicate this book to the Jesus Creed Community we host daily at www. jesuscreed.org. For three years we have conversed on this blog about nearly everything, and we are honored to say that, when it comes to blogs, there aren't many that exceed us in conversing in a way consistent with the Jesus Creed.

NOTES

DAY 2

9   *two kinds of love*   David W. Gill, *Doing Right* (Downers Grove, IL: IVP, 2004), 46.

DAY 5

26   *if you think me not irreverent*   C.S. Lewis, *Mere Christianity* (New York: Collier, 1960), 152.

DAY 10

48   *God walked through the labyrinth of promise*   This story is told in Genesis 15.

DAY 11

55   *It is a serious thing to live in a society of possible gods and goddesses*   C.S. Lewis, *The Weight of Glory and Other Addresses* (HarperSanFrancisco, 2001), 45, 46.

DAY 18

92   *remember the wrongdoer and the wrongdoing*   Miroslav Volf, *The End of Memory: Remembering Rightly in a Violent World* (Grand Rapids, MI: Eerdmans, 2006), 9.

93   *The memory of the Passion urges*   Volf, 125.

DAY 19

97   *The true indicator of spiritual well-being* John Ortberg, *The Life You've Always Wanted* (Grand Rapids, MI: Zondervan, 2002), 45.

DAY 20

102   *My father taught me to work*   I found this quotation in Al Gini, *The Importance of Being Lazy* (New York: Routledge, 2003), 15.

DAY 21

105   *Don't let the world around you squeeze you*   The New Testament in Modern English (Nashville: Thomas Nelson, 1997).

106   *Nine of ten young adults*   I take these statistics from David Kinnaman and Gabe Lyons, *unChristian: What a New Generation Really Thinks about Christianity . . . and Why it Matters* (Grand Rapids, MI: BakerBooks, 2007), 181–87.

DAY 25

126   *Dawn found her feet for the journey*   I borrow this story with permission from the publisher of my book *A Community Called Atonement* (Nashville: Abingdon, 2007), 3–4.

DAY 26

133   Philip Yancey, *What's So Amazing About Grace?* (Grand Rapids, MI: Zondervan, 1997).

134   *To say that God is love*   Frederick Buechner, *Beyond Words* (HarperSanFrancisco, 2004), 231.

DAY 27

138   *does not let wrongs . . . come to their fullest . . . expression* Karen Jobes, *1 Peter* (Grand Rapids, MI: Baker Books, 2005), 278.

DAY 29

148 *our life "before God adds up to zero"* Gordon Fee, *1 Corinthians* (Grand Rapids, MI: Eerdmans, 1987), 629.

DAY 31

158 *The passions blind us . . . only as we learn to love God* Roberta Bondi, *To Love as God Loves* (Philadelphia: Fortress, 1987), 65, 10.

160 *The true union with God is to do his will* François Fénelon, *Talking with God* (Brewster, MA: Paraclete Press, 1997), 11.

DAY 32

163 Cabell and Twain quotes from *The Yale Book of Quotations*, ed. Fred R. Shapiro (New Haven: Yale, 2006), 126, 780.

166 *an optimist is a guy that has never had much experience* *The Yale Book of Quotations*, 492.

DAY 38

191 *with honors suitable to her position* Robert Jewett, *Romans* (Minneapolis: Fortress, 2007), 945.

193 Lauren Winner, *Girl Meets God: On the Path to a Spiritual Life* (Chapel Hill: Algonquin Books, 2002); M. Teresa and B. Kolodiejchuk, *Mother Teresa: Come Be My Light* (New York: Doubleday, 2007); Virginia Stem Owens, *Caring for Mother: A Daughter's Long Goodbye* (Louisville, KY: Westminster John Knox, 2007).

DAY 39

197   *read as a lover reads*   Paul J. Griffiths, *Religious Reading* (New York: Oxford University Press, 1999), xi.

197   Eugene Peterson, *Eat This Book* (Grand Rapids, MI: Eerdmans, 2006).

40 Days Living the Jesus Creed

Fr. Kevin Maney

R ead each day's reflections in *40 Days Living the Jesus Creed* and then answer the corresponding questions as fully and completely as possible. As with anything else in life, what you get from this study will be commensurate with what you put into it. In fact, consider how your commitment to this study reflects your ability to live the Jesus Creed.

Ash Wednesday–Sunday (Lent Week 1)

1. Why is it important for us to remind ourselves daily that what is most important in our lives is our relationship with God and to love him? How was this reflected in ancient Israel? (Day 1)

2. What does it mean to love God with all your heart, soul, mind, and strength? Cite some practical examples of this love. How is this reflected in your own life? Share at least one example. Commit to reciting the Jesus Creed daily and be ready to report back to the group next week on how you did. (Day 1)

3. Why do you think Jesus amended the Shema? (Day 1)

4. Consider the areas of your life that Scot discusses in Day 2. Then assess how you are doing in these areas when it comes to loving God with heart, mind, soul, and strength. What are you doing well? Where do you need to improve? What can you do (or refrain from doing) that would help you improve the areas of your life you identified as needing improvement? (Day 2)

5. Read Luke 10:30–37. How would Scot's analysis of ancient Israel's "love of Torah" (p.14) affect Israel's call to be God's light to the world? Does the same hold true for us as Christians today? Why or why not? Who in your life do you need to work on being more neighborly to in the power of the Spirit? How do you propose to accomplish this? What, if anything, is holding you back? (Day 3)

6. Do you agree with Scot's claim that neighbor-love is unpredictable? Give personal examples to support your argument. What does it mean to respond to needs, not labels (pp. 16–17)? Cite some examples. How are you doing in this area? (Day 3)

7. Consider Scot's neighbor-love argument as a whole. Is it possible for neighbor-love to be or become unhealthy? If

so, how? If not, why? Provide some personal examples to support your argument. (Day 3)

8. How can your understanding of the hope and promise of new creation and being signs of Jesus light and love for the world impact your neighbor-love? How are both working (or not working) for you? (Day 3)

9. What does it mean to see God's face? When you gaze into the face of God, what do you see? When God gazes at your face, what do you think he sees, and how do you feel about that? When others gaze at you, do they see God's face reflected in you or something else? (Day 4)

10. What are some things that make you want to turn your face away from God? How can looking at God's face bring healing to you? *Make sure you can articulate this!* Why is your understanding of Jesus' death so critical to this gazing process? How might these considerations affect your ability to live the Jesus Creed each day? (Day 4)

11. What questions do you have about the Trinity? Why would some theologians call it the "dance of the Trinity" (p. 26)? (Day 5)

12. Read John 10:30, 38. What is another verb for dancing in the context of our relationship with God? How is your dancing with God going these days? What is going well? What needs to be improved? What kinds of things might make you a bad dancer and what might help you improve on your dance step? (Day 5)

Monday (Lent Week 1)–Sunday (Lent Week 2)

1. What are some ways we can love God, love ourselves, love others, and love God's good world? List some practical examples from your life. (Day 6)

2. What in yourself and your life hampers or prevents you from being God's *eikon*? What are some things you can do to rid yourself of those things you just identified? (Day 6)

3. Read Luke 15:11–32. Scot maintains that while we may give up on ourselves, God never does, and it is this kind of love that creates the Jesus Creed (p. 34). Think back on your life, past and present. In what ways, if any, have you given up on yourself? How has God demonstrated his faithfulness to you? Cite specific examples to illustrate this. (Day 7)

4. Given your answer to question 3, why is it appropriate for Christians to celebrate wildly as part of their faithful living? In what ways, if any, do you party like it is the eschaton (end time)? If you do not celebrate wildly, why don't you? (Day 7)

5. In what ways do you have a Missourian's heart? Explain. Do you agree with Scot that coming to the Table allows us to see God's face (p. 41)? When you come to the Table, do you see or experience God's presence? If so, how? If not, what do you see? (Day 8)

6. When, if at all, have you seen the face of God in others? If you have seen God's face in others, what did you see?

If others looked at you, would they readily see God's face or something else? Explain. (Day 8)

7. How is God's mercy lurking in the shadows of your life? Share some examples, if you are willing. (Day 9)

8. How are you embodying God's mercy to others? Cite some examples. Why do we need to first look at Jesus' face before we can embody God's mercy? (Day 9)

9. Read Genesis 15:1–12. How does this illustrate that God spoke to Abraham in Abraham's day and ways. How is God speaking likewise to you to demonstrate God's faithfulness? When you waiver about God's faithfulness, what Scripture verses do you turn to to help bolster your faith? Share with the group. (Day 10)

10. Scot argues that self-love is critical to living the Jesus Creed successfully. Does this surprise you? Why or why not? How can self-love become distorted? Assess the state of your self-love. What needs to be affirmed? What needs to be corrected? How do you propose to do that in a biblical way? Explain. (Day 11)

11. Do you agree with Scot that our inability to forgive ourselves distorts our ability to love ourselves? Why or why not? What are some ways you love yourself? Do these ways help or hinder you from embodying God's love for others? Explain. (Day 11)

12. Reflect on Psalm 139 (p. 57ff). As you reflect on God's intimate knowledge of you, what do you think he sees and knows about you? What needs to be healed? What needs to be affirmed? Make this the focus of your prayers this Lent (and beyond, if necessary). (Day 11)

13. Consider your family situation, whether it be your interactions with your spouse or children or someone else. How are you living the Jesus Creed with them? What are you doing well? What needs to be improved? Cite specific examples to illustrate your answers. How can you be strengthened to continue to love your family members as Jesus loves you? How can your interactions with family members be improved in a biblical manner? Explain. (Day 12)

Monday (Lent Week 2)–Sunday (Lent Week 3)

1. As Christians, we are called to give an account of our faith to others (cf. Colossians 4:5-6; 1 Peter 3:15). How would you respond to the list of criticisms in Dan Kimball's book (p. 65)? Resist the temptation to get defensive or self-righteous. How would you give an account to an outsider about your faith and why that person ought to come to your church regularly (or would you)? (Day 13)

2. Assess Scot's defense of the church. What do you find compelling? Not so compelling? Do you agree with him that reciting the Jesus Creed daily can be a balm for what ails the church? Why or why not? (Day 13)

3. Consider the people in your life. Are you missing any of the needy among them? If not, how are you addressing their needs? If so, in what ways can you address their needs? Do our examples have to be as spectacular as the one Scot gave on p. 72? Explain. (Day 14)

4. What are some things that prevent us from using our ears, eyes, and hands as Jesus would to address the needs of people around us? What, if anything, can we do to remove those obstacles? (Day 14)

5. Read Matthew 5:1–16. Do you agree with Scot that the Beatitudes are "a listing of the sorts of people who have found their way into the kingdom vision of Jesus, the sorts of people who love Jesus" (p. 78)? Why or why not? Would you be included in that list? If so, how? If not, what is holding you back? (Day 15)

6. How can loving others who live the Jesus Creed strengthen and encourage diversity in your church? Why is humility needed to do this? (Day 15)

7. Who has been an "influence for Jesus" on you and why? How are you being an influence for Jesus on others? ("I am not" is not an acceptable answer.) (Day 16)

8. Consider Scot's arguments about good works (pp. 82–84). What is your vision for your church in terms of being Jesus' salt and light? What must be done to make your vision a reality? (Day 16)

9. Scot's argument about our good works leading to God is crucially important (p. 84). Assess your own good works using his criteria. How do you stack up? Share as you are willing some concrete examples to support your assessment. (Day 16)

10. Consider carefully Scot's arguments about greatness in Jesus' eyes. Then on a scale of 1–10, with 10 being the top score, how do you think Jesus would rate your

greatness? What would be the basis for his rating? Provide some concrete examples. Then ask Jesus if he agrees with your assessment. What is he telling you? (Day 17)

11. Read Luke 6:27–36. Assess Scot's argument regarding enemy love. Is it biblical? Why or why not? What are its major strengths? Weaknesses? What, if anything, surprised you? Share stories of enemies you have loved by God's grace. (Day 18)

12. Who are the enemies in your life that God is calling you to love right now? How do you propose to go about that in light of Scot's arguments? Share with the group as you are willing. (Day 18)

13. Why is it essential to balance our good works with personal piety (spiritual disciplines) for successfully living the Jesus Creed? How are you doing with your spiritual disciplines? Where are you strong? What needs to improve and how do you plan to do that? (Day 19)

Monday (Lent Week 3)–Sunday (Lent Week 4)

1. Read Matthew 6:25–34 and then consider Scot's arguments regarding a life that is centered on God versus one that is not centered. How centered is your life? What are some tangible signs that it is or isn't? (Day 20)

2. Read Matthew 7:1–12. Assess Scot's arguments about judgmentalism. What do you agree with? Disagree with?

What is the difference between using good judgment and being judgmental? Between being judgmental and discerning? What do you consider to be the main antidote for judgmentalism? Explain. (Day 21)

3. Do you find Scot's suggestion surprising that sometimes we should withhold talking about Jesus with others? Why or why not? What are some examples from your life that might support or reject his argument? (Day 21)

4. Do you agree with Scot's definition of freedom? Why or why not? When you hear the words "live in the power of the Spirit," what comes to mind? How exactly do we do that? (Day 22)

5. Scot says that discipline has its place but is powerless to change lives (p. 115). Do you agree? Why or why not? In making this argument, isn't Scot simply arguing for another form of navel-gazing? Why or why not? (Day 22)

6. How exactly can loving others as yourself set you free? Cite some examples. (Day 22)

7. Read Romans 14. What is the difference between tolerance and love? What are some potential practical problems related to Scot's arguments about doing no wrong to the other (pp.118–19)? Think about the person(s) in your life who most irritate(s) you. Then consider Scot's argument that love engages the other. Why is living the Jesus Creed so difficult? (Day 23)

8. Using Scot's arguments about loving others, what are some practical ways you can show love to each other at your church? What might be some barriers or issues that make this difficult? (Day 23)

9. What are some of your memories that impact your current ministries and thoughts about living the Jesus Creed? How can personal memories serve to foster new ministries? Hinder them? Think back to Scot's argument about living in the Spirit. How might the Spirit's work play a healing role when it comes to our own personal memories? (Day 24)

10. Assess your church's treatment of the weak and poor. How are you doing? Provide some examples. In what ways can we improve? (Day 24)

11. What did you think and how did you feel when you read Dawn's story? Have you had a similar experience in which you washed Jesus' feet, either literally or metaphorically? If so, how did it make you feel? (Day 25)

12. How does Dawn's story illustrate the Jesus Creed in action? Do our acts always have to be this dramatic for us to live the Jesus Creed? Why or why not? (Day 25)

13. Read 1 John 4:7–21. When John and Scot talk about loving other Christians, do they have emotions in mind? Explain. Consider the saints of your church. Without naming names, who do you find easy to love and why? Who do you find hard to love and why? What insights about love and loving others does this provide you? (Day 26)

14. Now consider your relationship with God. What are some things in or about you that you think make it easy for God to love you? What are some things that might make it difficult for God to love you? How might this latter consideration affect the way you treat the "rascals" at your church? (Day 26)

Monday (Lent Week 4)–Sunday (Lent Week 5)

1. Besides reading the gospels regularly (you do read the gospels regularly, don't you?) what are some tangible ways you show your love for Jesus? For others? Cite specific examples to illustrate your point. (Day 27)

2. Think of times when your love for another member of the church or a person's love for you as a fellow member of the church covered a wrong done. Without naming names, how did you respond to that person's love for you (or how did that person respond to your love)? Be as specific as possible about the wrongs involved and how the love shown covered those wrongs. Was it hard to cover another person's wrong? Explain. (Day 27)

3. Read Acts 10. Consider the four principles Scot derives from it and apply them to your life. Have you ever been confronted with the opportunity to show boundary-crossing love? If so, what happened? If not, consider prayerfully what that might say about your ability to follow the Jesus Creed. (Day 28)

4. What are some things that help us keep our boundaries in place? Are there ever times or situations where we should not cross boundaries? Explain. (Day 28)

5. Read 1 Corinthians 12. In light of Scot's arguments in this chapter, why do we need love to drive the other gifts of the Spirit? Build your case on the basis of what Paul says about these gifts in 1 Corinthians 12. What are some of the gifts you share regularly with the

church and how are others benefited by your sharing of those gifts? (Day 29)

6. Consider Scot's argument that, "Real love . . . is what happens between two or more people in concrete reality." To illustrate what he is saying, Scot piggybacks his arguments with Paul's found in 1 Corinthians 13. "Love is patient [with others]; kind [to others]; and not envious [of others] or boastful [in front of others] or arrogant [in the face of others] or rude [to others]" (p. 153). Now assess your own ability to demonstrate love to other members of your church against these criteria. Citing concrete examples, what are you doing well? What needs to be improved? How do you propose to do that? (Day 30)

7. Continuing with his arguments related to 1 Corinthians 13, Scot claims that love orients us toward other people and then he talks about why self-denial is so necessary in this process (pp. 158–59). What would a life that is oriented toward others look like? When you think of self-denial, what comes to mind? When you think of denying yourself and following Jesus, what comes to mind? How are you doing in your ability to orient yourself toward others in your life, especially your church? Cite specific examples to illustrate your assessment. (Day 31)

8. Do you agree with Scot's statement that true love is optimistic (p. 163)? Why or why not? Compare and contrast the qualities of biblical optimism versus the world's optimism. If helpful, use the T-bar on the following page. Which, if any, do you possess more of?

If you don't have a biblical optimism that Scot talks about, what would it take for you to learn to develop it? (Day 32)

Biblical Optimism	Worldly Optimism

9. Assess Scot's argument that because love is the last word, i.e., it never ends, it produces a "love kind of life." What does that mean and what does that look like? How does your love for God and others measure up to this benchmark? Cite specific examples from your life to illustrate your answer. (Day 33)

10. Why must hope and giving logically flow from a life of love? Cite some examples from your life to illustrate your answer. (Day 33)

Monday (Lent Week 5)–Palm Sunday

1. Consider Scot's arguments about the temporary nature of gifts. Then consider the gifts God has given you. How do you use your gifts to establish that which will remain (love)? In other words, how do you use your gifts to build and nurture relationships, both inside and outside the church? Cite specific examples from your life. (Day 34)

2. When you think about the final consummation of pure Love, what comes to mind? Do you long for it? Why or why not? How might your answer illustrate Paul's assertion that we live in faith, hope, and love? (Day 35)

3. Do you agree or disagree with Scot's definition of faith (p. 176)? Why? What are some things you do that allows the Spirit to help you grow in faith? Assess the state of your faith right now. Consider specifically how it is (or isn't) transforming you in the power of the Spirit? Explain. What are some similarities you see between faith and hope? Differences? Explain. (Day 35)

4. Days 36–40 *focus on providing examples of the Jesus Creed love*. Answer the following questions with this controlling idea in mind. What does it mean to support the work of God? Cite specific examples of how you support Jesus and focus specifically on how you use your money to do that. How exactly does, "Supporting Jesus turn one's love for Jesus and his kingdom vision and for his followers into living reality" (p. 182)? Cite some examples. (Day 36)

5. Consider Scot's arguments about the Jesus Creed and money and then assess your church's stewardship of your money. How is it doing? Explain. (Day 36)

6. Consider Scot's definition of service in this chapter and then consider your own service, both inside and outside of your church. Do you like to serve? Why or why not? How would you rate your service (no false modesty, please)? What do you do well? What needs to improve? What's holding you back from implementing improvements? (Day 37)

7. Do you agree that love must affirm others? Why or why not? Compare and contrast worldly affirmations with Jesus Creed love affirmations (use the T-bar on the following page if that helps you). What are some essential similarities? Differences? (Day 38)

8. Consider Scot's argument that "affirmation requires the willingness to dethrone our own egos" (p. 190) and then consider your own willingness to affirm others. Does your ego need to be dethroned? Why or why not? Cite some specific examples from your life to illustrate your answer. Resolve to affirm someone in your life each day this coming week and then reflect on how well you were able to keep your resolution. Talk about this with someone you trust. (Day 38)

9. Read Matthew 3:1–12. Scot suggests that it was John's love for God that led him to speak of Jesus. Is this what comes to mind when you read these verses, especially his words to the Pharisees and Sadducees? Why or why not? (Day 38)

Worldly Affirmation	JCL Affirmation

10. Consider carefully Scot's arguments about using our voice to point to Jesus. How are you doing in this regard? What are you doing well? What's holding you back? Cite specific examples to illustrate your answer. (Day 39)

11. Do you agree that you need to read about Jesus until the gospels' words about him saturate your bones? Why or why not? Do you do this regularly? Why or why not? If you don't, what is holding you back and what do you need in order to get started? (Day 39)

12. How do you typically fail to live the Jesus Creed. Cite some examples. What, if anything, are you doing about this? Do you struggle to receive grace? Why or why not? (Day 40)

13. Consider the pattern of Jesus Creed grace (p. 202). What can happen if grace doesn't follow rebuke? If grace is offered without rebuke? How are you doing in imitating Jesus' pattern of offering grace to others? In accepting it from others? Cite some examples. (Day 40)

ABOUT PARACLETE PRESS

Who We Are

Paraclete Press is a publisher of books, recordings, and DVDs on Christian spirituality. Our publishing represents a full expression of Christian belief and practice—from Catholic to Evangelical, from Protestant to Orthodox.

We are the publishing arm of the Community of Jesus, an ecumenical monastic community in the Benedictine tradition. As such, we are uniquely positioned in the marketplace without connection to a large corporation and with informal relationships to many branches and denominations of faith.

What We Are Doing

PARACLETE PRESS BOOKS | Paraclete publishes books that show the richness and depth of what it means to be Christian. Although Benedictine spirituality is at the heart of all that we do, we publish books that reflect the Christian experience across many cultures, time periods, and houses of worship. We publish books that nourish the vibrant life of the church and its people.

We have several different series, including the best-selling Paraclete Essentials and Paraclete Giants series of classic texts in contemporary English; Voices from the Monastery—men and women monastics writing about living a spiritual life today; award-winning poetry; best-selling gift books for children on the occasions of baptism and first communion; and the Active Prayer Series that brings creativity and liveliness to any life of prayer.

MOUNT TABOR BOOKS | Paraclete's newest series, Mount Tabor Books, focuses on liturgical worship, art and art history, ecumenism, and the first millennium church; and was created in conjunction with the Mount Tabor Ecumenical Centre for Art and Spirituality in Barga, Italy.

PARACLETE RECORDINGS | From Gregorian chant to contemporary American choral works, our recordings celebrate the best of sacred choral music composed through the centuries that create a space for heaven and earth to intersect. Paraclete Recordings is the record label representing the internationally acclaimed choir Gloriæ Dei Cantores, praised for their "rapt and fathomless spiritual intensity" by American Record Guide; the Gloriæ Dei Cantores Schola, specializing in the study and performance of Gregorian chant; and the other instrumental artists of the Gloriæ Dei Artes Foundation.

Paraclete Press is also privileged to be the exclusive North American distributor of the recordings of the Monastic Choir of St. Peter's Abbey in Solesmes, France, long considered to be a leading authority on Gregorian chant.

PARACLETE VIDEO | Our DVDs offer spiritual help, healing, and biblical guidance for a broad range of life issues including grief and loss, marriage, forgiveness, facing death, bullying, addictions, Alzheimer's, and spiritual formation.

Learn more about us at our website:
www.paracletepress.com or phone us
toll-free at 1.800.451.5006

SCAN
TO
READ
MORE

You may be interested in The Jesus Creed series....

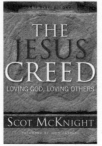

The Jesus Creed
LOVING GOD, LOVING OTHERS

Winner
of the 2005
*Christianity
Today* Book
Award

ISBN: 978-1-55725-400-9
Paperback, $16.99

Love God with all your heart, soul, mind, and strength, but also love others as yourselves. Discover how the Jesus Creed of love for God and others can transform your life.

And for groups studying the Jesus Creed...

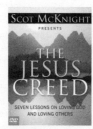

The Jesus Creed
THE DVD—SEVEN LESSONS ON
LOVING GOD AND LOVING OTHERS

ISBN: 978-1-55725-619-5 | DVD, 50 minutes

The perfect tool for groups of all kinds, this DVD provides an engaging seven-week study.

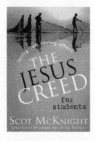

The Jesus Creed for Students
LOVING GOD, LOVING OTHERS

ISBN: 978-1-55725-883-0 | Paperback, $13.99

Essential Christian formation for anyone between the ages of 16 and 22.

Scot McKnight has worked the Jesus Creed out with high school and college students, seeking to show how this double commandment to love makes sense and gives shape to the moral lives of young adults. *The Jesus Creed for Students* aims to demonstrate a simple truth—that followers of Jesus really follow Jesus. (Also, it's practical, filled with stories, and backed up and checked by youth pastors.)

Available from most booksellers or through Paraclete Press:
www.paracletepress.com | 1-800-451-5006.
Try your local bookstore first.